HEARTS THAT TURN

GENERATIONS PREPARING THE
WAY OF THE LORD TOGETHER!

HEARTS THAT TURN

PATRICIA KING
WITH BENJAMIN DEITRICK
FOREWORD BY BARBARA YODER

Hearts that Turn
© 2023 Patricia King Enterprises

All Rights Reserved. No part of this publication may be reproduced, stored in a retrieval system or transmitted in any form or by any means – electronic, mechanical, photocopy, recording or any other – without the prior written permission of the author.

Unless otherwise identified, scripture quotations are taken from the the New King James Version®. Copyright© 1982 by Thomas Nelson. Used by permission. All rights reserved.

Scripture quotations marked (NASB) are taken from NEW AMERICAN STANDARD BIBLE®, Copyright© 1960, 1962, 1963, 1968, 1971, 1972, 1973, 1975, 1977, by The Lockman Foundation. Used by permission. Scripture quotations marked NASB1995 are taken from the NEW AMERICAN STANDARD BIBLE® 1995 revision.

Scripture quotations marked (AMPC) are taken from the Amplified Bible, Classic Edition, Copyright© 1954, 1958, 1962, 1964, 1965, 1987 by The Lockman Foundation.

Scripture quotations marked (NIV) are taken from the Holy Bible, New International Version®, NIV® Copyright© 1973, 1978, 1984, 2011 by Biblica, Inc.® Used by permission. All rights reserved worldwide.

Scripture quotations marked (ESV) are taken from The Holy Bible, English Standard Version. ESV® Text Edition: 2016. Copyright© 2001 by Crossway Bibles, a publishing ministry of Good News Publishers.

Scripture quotations marked (KJV) are taken from King James Version, public domain.

ISBN: 978-1-62166-538-0

Patricia King Ministries
PO Box 1017
Maricopa, AZ 85139

ENDORSEMENTS

The blessing of God is spilling out on the generations, causing many *Hearts that Turn* back to the ways of God! This excellent book is full of biblical insights that can unite the generations for the great end-time revival. Read it and be ready for your heart to be changed. And get a few extra copies to share with your friends, young and old.

Brian Simmons
The Passion Translation

My heart was on fire as I read this beautiful work! Patricia and Benjamin have gifted this generation with spiritual language and practical wisdom that it desperately needs as we all navigate spiritual leadership and the challenges that it can often bring. The need for unity, love, and humility has never been greater, and I'm beyond grateful to know that these two spiritual leaders model all of this so well. Open up your heart as you read *Hearts that Turn,* and get ready to receive revelation, healing, and vision.

Jeremiah Johnson
Bestselling Author
Senior Leader of The Ark Fellowship
The Altar Global, and The Altar School

My dear friend Patricia King has done it again. Ever sensitive to the voice of the Holy Spirit, she has prophetically captured the word of the Lord for this season and gracefully distilled it into a book that will catalyze breakthrough in your life. Take this message to heart, run with it, and watch what God does.

Dr. Ché Ahn
Senior Leader
Harvest Rock Church, Pasadena, CA
President, Harvest International Ministry

International Chancellor, Wagner UniversityWhat an excellent—and necessary—book! Filled with godly wisdom from two generations, *Hearts that Turn* will help all generations work together to achieve their prophetic mandate in this critical hour of kingdom history (Malachi 4:5-6). Completing the practical Conversation Points and Application sections at the end of every chapter will ensure that each reader will go away changed—and families, communities, and nations will reap the results.

Wesley & Stacey Campbell
Shiloh Global Ministries

I have known Patricia King for decades. One of the beautiful things, among the many, about Patricia's life, is her passion for the next generation. She makes room for them at every level. She celebrates the breakthroughs. She has the hard conversations. She hosts the conferences that let their voices shine in the earth as she sits back with her tender smile, like a true spiritual mama. This is the way in which she has walked for years, bringing the next generation right alongside her and watching them spring forth in their own divine calling. What makes an even greater impact in our hearts is the co-writer of this book—a next-generation leader, Benjamin Deitrick. So I would say, if you want to know what God is doing in the earth right now between generations—get this book. Read this book. Walk out this book. That is exactly what I will be doing.

Julie Meyer
Author: 30 Days Of Praying The Psalms
& Singing The Scriptures
Intotheriver.net

A generational turning of hearts and an orphan spirit are such crucial subjects that God made sure that He addressed these topics before 400 years of silence ... That's serious! These concepts are crucial for the end times and for the intended harvest of the ages. In this generation, father wounds are prevalent and responsible for more immoral behavior and broken identity than anything else.

Hearts that Turn is a field manual for everything from spiritual fathers and mothers to orphaned hearts to mentorship. This book is filled with solid principles, wisdom, revelation, and hope. We highly recommend *Hearts that Turn* as well as anything that Patricia King is a part of.

Sean and Christa Smith
www.seanandchristasmith.com
Speakers, Authors
Co-host of "Keep It 100
w/ Sean & Christa Smith" podcast

Patricia King is well-known as an apostolic mama to so many in the body of King Jesus. When I heard she had written a book on the move of God in our supernatural family, I knew it was a "right now" word for what God is doing. Her revelation of the covenant Kingdom family brings a new lens to the family altar. I'm excited about this!

Troy Brewer
Senior Pastor, Open Door Church, Burleson, TX
Bestselling Author
Founding Director of Redemption Ranch

Patricia King and Benjamin Deitrick have put together something special. Their book, *Hearts that Turn*, is filled with revelation about the power released when the generations run together. These pages overflow with impartation that will position you to take part in the coming move of God. There is more than information in these pages, there is spiritual substance, because Patricia and Benjamin have not only written about the generations running together, they have lived it.

Robert Hotchkin
Robert Hotchkin Ministries
Men on the Frontlines
RobertHotchkin.com

Dedicated to

Our Heavenly Father, who longs for the generations
to turn their hearts to Him and each other
&
Those who are willing to fulfill His desire

Table of Contents

Foreword / by Barbara Yoder 13

Introduction / The Turning of Hearts 19
    Benjamin Deitrick

Chapter 1 / In the Beginning, God 25
    Patricia King

Chapter 2 / Spiritual Fathers and Mothers, Arise 37
    Patricia King

Chapter 3 / Five Key Attributes of Spiritual Parents 51
    Patricia King

Chapter 4 / Avoiding Codependence and Guilt Trips 65
    Patricia King

Chapter 5 / Mentors and Leaders 77
    Patricia King and Benjamin Deitrick

Chapter 6 / What Is a Spiritual Child? 89
    Benjamin Deitrick

Chapter 7 / Five Important Attributes of Spiritual Children 101
    Benjamin Deitrick

Chapter 8 / Generations Growing in Relationship 117
    Patricia King

Chapter 9 / Questions and Responses 131
    Patricia King and Benjamin Deitrick

Chapter 10 / The Joys of Being a Spiritual Father, Mother, Son or
Daughter 145
Various Authors

Chapter 11 / There's Healing in His Wings 159
Patricia King and Benjamin Deitrick

Concluding Remarks 169

FOREWORD

Barbara Yoder

I'll never forget my first meeting with Patricia King. It was in Torquay, England where we both were speaking at the same conference. I was looking forward to meeting "the real Patricia King."

As we sat around the lunch table in the green room with Susan Davies and Claire Moody, UK leaders for Patricia's ministry, the atmosphere was alive with spirited conversation and laughter. I liked Patricia. I felt an instant connection. I quickly gained great respect for her as a leader and for her authenticity as a radical lover and follower of Jesus.

I was amazed at the extent of her entrepreneurial leadership. She had developed several impactful and ongoing ministries that were changing lives as well as changing the face of how we do ministry today. She is one of the pioneers of Internet Church, ministering to many around the world. To say the least, her accomplishments were impressive. But more than that, she held to her core values of God first, listening to His voice, immersing herself in His Word, and following Him with her whole heart. Flowing out of that was a heart of love and redemption coupled with a passionate cry for reconciling mercy.

I believe reconciliation is one of her primary mantles. It was out of her own experience of huge relational fractures that forced her into a learning curve of how to restore them. And she worked at it until she was successful. Shipwrecked relationships can be restored.

When we first met, she was in the beginning of becoming a champion for the younger generation; that generation where many had been lost amid fractured family relationships, faulty belief systems, injustices, and a multitude of issues. Yet it was a generation that was both zealous to enter into and succeed in ministry because of their deep love for the Lord. Some, even though they faced many challenges, were committed to moving forward to fulfill their destiny. She invited them into her sphere without judgment, helping them to find the path forward. Her willingness to champion their development and success with and for GOD was impressive.

It was within this context that she asked me recently if I would write the foreword for this book. Patricia was in the middle of mediating a ministry relationship that had imploded, one with an older leader and a younger leader. Those leaders were me, Barbara Yoder, a seasoned apostolic leader, and Benjamin Deitrick, a gifted and anointed millennial minister who led our church for a number of years and has contributed valuable insights, revelations, and teachings to this book. Benjamin and I had been working in ministry together for many years, initially to model how the generations work together, when we came under attack, ending suddenly in a tragic and painful broken relationship.

When you are inside an attack such as we experienced, you cannot always see clearly. We were both hit with disbelief, shock, anger, depression, and the challenge to forgive. This is where it helps to have someone objective operating in love and faith for both parties to help the process.

Too often, in the midst of relational assaults, we nurse our personal wounds and justify our offense without giving attention to the bigger picture. The enemy wants divisions, factions, and broken relationships. If we are not committed to a healthy process of healing and restoration, those who are close to the situation and those observing the conflicts all suffer as well. We see this often in the case of broken marriages that terminate in divorce. The children suffer and are often forced to take sides, which promotes further division and brokenness. Malachi prophesied that if there is not a turning of hearts, then curse comes to the land. This is a grievous consequence indeed.

Months following the original fallout, God whispered to me, "To have authority in the ministry of reconciliation, you have to overcome this breach." In our individual painful paths forward, we longed to overcome. We understood that if we fought the battle well, then God could release an unusual and powerful mantle of reconciliation that would fall on Benjamin (representing younger generation leaders) and me (representing older generation leaders).

Paul said in 2 Corinthians 5:18 that God reconciled us to Himself through Christ and gave us the ministry of reconciliation.

That reconciliation took place through Christ's death on the cross—and it will take the embracing of the cross in our lives today—to bring about His ongoing ministry of reconciliation in our midst. It's that ministry that so many of us in the body of Christ don't always do well.

As Benjamin and I were encouraged to process honestly and vulnerably with one another, I came to personally perceive the high degree of misunderstanding that drove the parting of ways. In addition to other dynamics, there had been a lack of clear communication and listening carefully to each other's hearts, which contributed to the attack on the relationship.

I was very blindsided by what happened, as was Benjamin, and reconciliation seemed like an impossibility initially. However, it was that nudge from God that spoke to me, "You must see this one all the way through, and furthermore, you must model reconciliation." Those nudges kept my heart focused on the goal in the midst of my personal heart trauma and loss. Benjamin was going through a similar awakening. We had to ultimately make a decision to reach toward the prize, one part of the high calling in Christ Jesus, the call to reconciliation. His broken body needed healing.

There was a process that began with Benjamin and me, and at the time of this writing, one that we are still engaged in, fully walking out various levels of the breakthrough. The grief process cannot be rushed. There are always real challenges but also real breakthroughs and victories. In order to find peace with God and man, we must learn to follow the path of forgiveness and work through every challenge until the peace of God and the heart of

God permeates our lives. Too often, breaches remain just that: breaches. If the generations are going to make it together and labor beside one another for kingdom advancement, we must commit to fully love God, His Word, those we're in conflict with, and the process.

Amid our season of deep pain and confusion, we committed to a journey of healing. According to Malachi 4:5–6, I had to take personal responsibility to turn my heart back to Benjamin, and in the midst of his wounding and devastation, his heart was called to turn back to me.

We are currently, patiently, through grace walking out the process and invitation laid out in this book. It has required both of us to sit down and hear each other's perspectives. We chose to be open, honest, and gracious with each other, sharing how we perceive each side of the story without accusation or argumentativeness. I have appreciated Benjamin's posture of honor and patience in this process.

When we chose to turn our hearts to each other, a pathway to healing and peace began. Benjamin and I both committed to the end goal of reconciliation. We might not even understand at this time what that fully looks like on every level that was affected, but we are confident that God was in Christ, reconciling the world back to Himself. And now we have the amazing opportunity to learn to walk out the heart of God and the Word of God with the generations.

I salute Patricia as a mother in the faith, and I champion Benjamin who with me is committed to overcoming the spiritual assaults targeting intergenerational leaders. Patricia, Benjamin, and I stand together as those who have penned in this book some of the insights we learned and are learning in our journey.

For the sake of the healing of the Body, we are committed to sharing openly with you. I trust that the vulnerable disclosures in this foreword will give you, too, the faith and courage to embrace opportunities to reconcile with those you have experienced conflict with.

We are in that "Elijah Mandate" time as prophesied in Malachi 4:5-6. May God use this book to help believers and leaders, old and young, step over the line and take the risk required to turn our hearts to each other and *together* prepare the way of the Lord in the midst of a very dark hour. The greatest outpouring of God's glory is at hand—let's serve Him with one heart, exalting Him together in the purity of love and true worship.

Introduction

THE TURNING OF HEARTS

Benjamin Deitrick

> Behold, I will send you Elijah the prophet
> Before the coming of the great and dreadful
> day of the Lord.
> And he will turn
> The hearts of the fathers to the children,
> And the hearts of the children to their fathers,
> Lest I come and strike the earth with a curse.
>
> *Malachi 4:5–6*

Malachi 4:5–6 are the last two verses before the New Testament, and they set a clear picture of what was to come. Before the Messiah's coming, an Elijah anointing would be released to prepare the way of the Lord. Isaiah described it when he declared that every valley would be raised, every mountain brought low, every crooked place made straight, and more (Isaiah 40:3-5). It was a season of reordering and preparation, removing every obstacle for the glory of the Lord—manifested in the coming Messiah.

Elijah walked in this anointing as one man in his day. He was sent to the people of Israel to prepare them for the glory of the Lord, with the main assignment to confront and remove idolatry. Jesus referred to John the Baptist as Elijah who "was to come again" if people could receive it (Matthew 11:14). John the Baptist also walked alone in this anointing. In our time, this same anointing is present and will continually increase until the full manifestation of Jesus Christ is again revealed—this time, as Lord and Judge of all the earth.

In this hour, the anointing to prepare the way for Christ rests not on merely one individual, but rather on an entire generation—everyone alive on the earth who will say "yes" and partner with the purposes of the Lord. Through Christ, the mantle, spirit, and power of Elijah are within us, and they must be released through us to see the glory of the Lord revealed in power and strength.

There is a qualifying factor, a key ingredient that is needed to see the release of this anointing through the Body of Christ. This key ingredient is *the turning of hearts one to another* as fathers, mothers, sons, and daughters. Yet, there are many giants standing in the way of this happening.

When we look at our world today, we can see a pandemic of epic proportions—it is a virus of the soul. Fatherlessness runs rampant in our communities, and broken homes and families are everywhere. Selfishness is the theme of our day, and the god of

> **In this hour, the anointing to prepare the way of Christ rests not on merely one individual, but rather on an entire generation—everyone alive on the earth who will say "yes" and partner with the purposes of the Lord.**

self has truly been exalted in every facet of our society. We are reaping the fruit of that idolatry.

It is easy to see the "curse" that comes from hearts not turning, as mentioned in Malachi. It takes zero discernment to see that we have entire generations that seem "lost" in confusion and rebellion and who are engaged in every kind of sin. We see the generations walking in offense and great division instead of a unity that turns one's heart to another and thus, transforms the world.

It is important to note that in these verses, not only is Elijah mentioned, but in verse four, it says to "remember the law of Moses." When Jesus manifested to the world, He came full of grace and truth and was the perfect embodiment of both. He was and is the fulfillment of both the Law and the Prophets, which Moses and Elijah represent. We see this even on the Mount of Transfiguration in Luke 9:28-36. The coming of Elijah is preceded by a "remembrance" of the ways and law of God—His covenant commandments and promises that were honored and fulfilled through Christ. We live in a time when every bastion of these covenant witnesses is under siege.

The enemy is fighting as hard as he can against this unity because he knows the ramifications to his kingdom if the church truly gets a hold of this in a healthy way. Satan's kingdom would crumble! So, he is throwing every last dart he can to keep us divided and in pain through misunderstandings, distorted communication, and our own self-exaltation. This isn't simply about young and old coming together, this is about the culmination of all the ages. Once it is expressed fully, the unity, love, and maturity of the Body will prepare the way for the coming of the Lord. The situation today is dire. If ever we needed an Elijah anointing, it is now! We must turn!

In the Hebrew language, the word "turn" used in Malachi 4 is *shub* (phonetic: shoob). It means to "turn back or return." It can even mean to retreat. I find this very interesting. We often think of "retreat" as failure or defeat when, in fact, it can be a strategic move in the art of warfare. If you retreat, you are basically acknowledging that the enemy you are fighting is too strong for you in the current way you are engaging with him. In other words, what you're doing isn't effective. I believe this is a prophetic picture to show us that just one generation fighting the enemy or advancing the Kingdom on their own is not going to win the victory. We have been fighting on our own in many ways, each generation in their own corner, thinking they know best. What if we retreated not to give up or give in to the enemy, but rather to regroup and reform as ONE army and then reengage the enemy to rout him!?

The Bible clearly says that Elijah is who will turn the hearts of the fathers to the sons and vice versa. In other words, this isn't something we can make happen in our own strength or with the arm of the flesh. That will never work. It's not a formula. It's organic and living, something birthed by the Spirit of God. He will do this work, and He will cause all of us to turn toward one another for the strategic purpose to prepare the way of the Lord.

As you delve into the chapters of this book, open your heart. We, who are writing, don't assume to have it "all together" or even attempt to know everything about this subject. The book is a prophetic heart cry and an invitation to a conversation on a subject that we believe is vital to grasp and walk in from a heart perspective and motive as we *advance together to prepare the way of the Lord.*

Chapter One

IN THE BEGINNING, GOD

Patricia King

"In the beginning God created the heavens and the earth" – *Genesis 1:1*

In the beginning was the Word,
and the Word was with God,
and the Word was God.
He was in the beginning with God.
All things were made through Him,
and without Him
nothing was made that was made.
In Him was life, and the life was the light of men.
John 1:1-4

What a mess the world is in—conflict and crisis are everywhere! Political upheavals, racial tensions, economic uncertainties, corruption, lawlessness, wars and rumors of wars, natural disasters, and opposition to biblical values, morals, and faith are just a few of the tense issues of this hour. These types of curses and consequences come when we live contrary to God's ways and plans, but blessings come when we realign with Him. If we submit to God's divine order in this season, we can overcome every hindrance, obstacle, and curse. This current season can potentially be the finest hour for the church as we arise and shine, bringing light into the darkness. Kings and nations can come to the brightness of our rising, and a billion-soul harvest can be reaped for the glory and honor of the Lord. What a victory!

One of the key elements to experiencing this overcoming victory is the turning of the hearts of the generations back to each other: fathers to children and children to fathers.

The prophetic word of the Lord in Malachi 4:5-6, calling generations to run together, is a very clear emphasis in this hour. However, in society today, it is not uncommon to hear of natural fathers and mothers forsaking their children—even taking their lives in the womb before they ever have a chance to live out a day of their destiny. The foster care system is overloaded with neglected, abused, and abandoned children, and more families are needed to adopt children who have been signed into the system, often at birth.

Children are often resistant to their parents and purpose to make their own choices regarding matters such as sexual and gender preferences and identity. In the United States, a minor may petition the court seeking to divorce his parents.

Similar core issues of conflict, neglect, abuse, and abandonment are also found in the church when observing spiritual parents and children. We are broken. We need help.

> **This current season can potentially be the finest hour for the church as we arise and shine, bringing light into the darkness.**

The Lord spoke the solution to breaking this curse in Malachi as He called the hearts of the fathers—parents—to turn to the children, and then the children to the parents. When the parents turn their hearts, then the children will follow. This prophetic call is for both natural and spiritual parents and children. However, in this book, we will focus on the spiritual. In an hour where there is a clear transition of eras and the passing of the baton from one generation to another, this prophetic call is even more critical and relevant.

Our Expectation

We all experience an internal expectation in our soul to be fathered and mothered. Most individuals also have a natural desire to give birth to children and raise them. Even though these longings are natural and God-given, it is important that we first, and above all else, acknowledge God Himself in all things. That is why the first commandment in the Old Testament was "You shall have no other gods before Me" (Exodus 20:3). In the New Testament, Jesus taught that the following commandment was the greatest, "You shall love the Lord your God with all your heart, with all your soul, and with all your mind" (Matthew 22:37–38.

When we acknowledge God first, then His blessing will fill the relationships that follow. If we honor God first as our Father, then when He blesses us with individuals who carry His parental heart for us, we will see them as a true gift and not an idol. Divine order always produces divine glory.

God First

In the beginning, there was God. There was no earth, sun, moon, stars, land, oceans, trees, or animals until He created them. Everything came from Him, by Him, and through Him. He is our source—the source of all.

His desire was for children, so He created humankind in His image and likeness. While the cows, fish, shrubs, birds, and planets were all created by God, they were not in His image and likeness, as we are. We are like Him. Just like when you give birth to children, they resemble you, we resemble God. We came from Him.

The God of all power and authority blessed us to be fruitful, to multiply, to fill the earth and steward it, and to have dominion in the earth. All of this was given to us, but it originated from Him.

Genesis 1:27–28

> So God created man in His own image; in the image of God He created him; male and female He created them. Then God blessed them, and God said to them, "Be fruitful and multiply; fill the earth and subdue it; have dominion over the fish of the sea, over the birds of the air, and over every living thing that moves on the earth."

Male and Female – Father and Mother

God created humankind in His image—male and female. The dominant gender used in scripture to describe God is male, and He is called Father, not Mother. However, in Him are both male and female and father and mother. We see through the account of creation that God created Adam (meaning 'human') by forming him from the dust of the ground and then breathing His breath of life into him. He then became a living soul.

God then took a rib from Adam and created Eve. Thus, both male and female were in God and in the original Adam. Then woman was taken from Adam—man.

Genesis 2:21-23

And the LORD God caused a deep sleep to fall on Adam, and he slept; and He took one of his ribs, and closed up the flesh in its place.

Then the rib which the LORD God had taken from man He made into a woman, and He brought her to the man.

And Adam said:

"This is now bone of my bones
And flesh of my flesh;
She shall be called Woman,
Because she was taken out of Man.

In God is all you need for life. If you need a father, He is a Father. If you need a mother, He also is a Mother. He is Friend, Brother, Wisdom, Healer, Savior, King, Provider, and Comforter. He is everything! Before we can have healthy relationships with others, we must acknowledge God as our first source of all things.

Then we can be grateful and joyful for those He uses in our lives to reveal various aspects of His being and blessings.

In the following chapters, we will share about spiritual fathers and mothers. It is an essential understanding to acknowledge God as our primary relationship of both Father and Mother so we are free to enjoy the blessings of the individuals in our lives through whom He chooses to reveal Himself.

God's Maternal Nature

As aforementioned, God is not directly referred to in scripture as Mother, but many portions of the Bible speak of His maternal love and nature. Let's confirm this.

For example, one of the images we see in scripture is that of a mother bird covering her children under her wings.

Matthew 23:37

O Jerusalem, Jerusalem, the one who kills the prophets and stones those who are sent to her! How often I wanted to gather your children together, as a hen gathers her chicks under *her* wings, but you were not willing!

Deuteronomy 32:10–11

He found him in a desert land
And in the wasteland, a howling wilderness;
He encircled him, He instructed him,
He kept him as the apple of His eye.
As an eagle stirs up its nest,
Hovers over its young,

Spreading out its wings, taking them up,
Carrying them on its wings.

Psalm 57:1

Be merciful to me, O God, be merciful to me!
For my soul trusts in You;
And in the shadow of Your wings I will make my refuge,
Until these calamities have passed by.

Psalm 91:4

He shall cover you with His feathers,
And under His wings you shall take refuge.

We also find the example of God describing Himself with the nature of a mother bear.

Hosea 13:8a (NIV)

Like a bear robbed of her cubs,
I will attack them and rip them open.

We further see Him described through the example of a responsible, caring, and comforting mother.

Isaiah 66:12–13

For thus says the Lord …
"As one whom his mother comforts,
So I will comfort you;
And you shall be comforted in Jerusalem."

Isaiah 49:15–16

"Can a woman forget her nursing child,
And not have compassion on the son of her womb?
Surely they may forget,
Yet I will not forget you.
See, I have inscribed you on the palms of My hands;
Your walls are continually before Me.

God Has First Place

God is the Beginning and the End—the Alpha and the Omega. He is the progenitor of all things, and if you acknowledge Him first as all you need, you will never be disappointed or set up for failure. He is more than enough. Establishing God as first in your life is setting divine order in place, preparing you for great blessings.

Many today look for spiritual fathers and mothers and are disappointed when these individuals are non-existent, passive, imperfect, or negligent. If our trust is in God to be everything we need, we will not suffer disappointments like this.

Israel Wanted a King

In the time when God appointed prophets to proclaim His ways and judges to enforce them, His people told the prophet, Samuel, that they wanted a king like the other nations. They failed to acknowledge that God was their King—and the best one ever!

Samuel was grieved over their request and went to God. The Lord told him to reveal to the people what would happen if they were given a king other than God. He submitted a list of failures, abusive behaviors, and disturbing consequences to them. You'd think that would be enough to cause a change of heart, but no. This was their response:

> "No, but we will have a king over us, that we also may be like all the nations, and that our king may judge us and go out before us and fight our battles" (1 Samuel 8:19–20).

Their request was so absurd! God was their King, and He caused them to win their battles, but unfortunately, He was not their first love or consideration. They wanted to exchange Him for a human king, and a dysfunctional king at that… and this is exactly what they got—King Saul!

We can never exchange God for someone or something else. In every area of our lives, He is the source of all we need, and we are to acknowledge Him in all things.

Proverbs 3:5–6
Trust in the Lord with all your heart,
And lean not on your own understanding;
In all your ways acknowledge Him,
And He shall direct your paths.

It is vital that we wholeheartedly acknowledge that God + Nothing = Everything we need. Parents can fail us or fall short in their duties, but God does not. Children can fail and disappoint us, but God does not. Our trust is to be in Him alone.

GOD + NOTHING = EVERYTHING WE NEED

He is the perfect Father (Mother) and the perfect Son (Daughter). He will help us be quality and treasured spiritual fathers or mothers because His paternal and maternal nature is in us. He will also allow us to be blessed and cherished spiritual sons or daughters because His sonship (daughtership) lives within us.

Never an Orphan

Many today suffer from what is referred to as an orphan spirit. The afflicted individual believes they lack care, belonging, and identity. They are constantly looking to be validated but are seldom confident or secure. They grieve because they lack people in their lives who will spiritually parent them.

The following are some of the symptoms that the orphan spirit produces:

1. Feeling Distant from God
2. Insecurity
3. Lack of Confidence
4. Poverty Mindset – there is never enough to satisfy.
5. Competitiveness
6. Jealousy
7. Striving
8. Performance Pressure
9. Trouble with Trusting
10. Difficulty with Authority

11. Unfulfilled Dreams

12. Subject to Addiction and Compulsive Behaviors

13. Depression

14. Difficulty Completing Assignments

15. Lack of Belonging

When you believe God is everything you need, you do not trust in the arm of flesh although you can appreciate and honor everyone He brings into your life. God will fill and heal every area of your life where people have failed you if you allow Him to be your Father, Mother, Teacher, Healer, Deliverer, and Guide. If He brings others into your life to model some of His attributes and offer you human interaction and affirmation, you will be blessed. But you will also be blessed if He doesn't. You are never an orphan when God is everything you need. You are never an orphan when you receive and acknowledge God as your all!

Hearts Turning

Malachi prophesied the hearts of the fathers turning to the children and the children's hearts turning to the fathers. He further prophesied that if hearts did not turn, then the land would be cursed. Today we see evidence of a measure of this curse. We need the curse to be broken and to come into fresh alignment with the Lord. The turning of the hearts of the generations to one another is important for the breaking of this curse, but what is more important is that we first trust Him fully and acknowledge that He is the source of all we need.

The Lord is coming soon for a Bride who has made herself ready. Let's prepare by turning our hearts fully toward Him and then to one another.

CONVERSATION POINT

Discuss the importance of putting God first in all things and highlight areas where we have fallen short in society and in the church.

ACTIVATION

1. Ask Holy Spirit to convict you of any areas where you have gone to others before you have gone to God and where you have felt you needed others more than Him. If He brings anything to mind, repent, receive forgiveness and cleansing (according to 1 John 1:9).

2. Pray the following prayer, acknowledging God as your Father.

   Heavenly Father,

   I acknowledge You as the Giver of my life. You are the One who formed and fashioned me and filled me with destiny and purpose. You have watched over and celebrated me from the moment I was conceived to this very hour. You are my Father, and You care for me with unchanging and unconditional love. You are all I need, and You will withhold no good thing from me. Everything good comes from You.

   I love You and honor You with all my heart and life, Amen.

Chapter Two

SPIRITUAL FATHERS AND MOTHERS, ARISE

Patricia King

Jesus taught the following in Matthew 23:8-11, "But do not be called Rabbi; for One is your Teacher, and you are all brothers. Do not call *anyone* on earth your father; for One is your Father, He who is in heaven. Do not be called leaders; for One is your Leader, *that is*, Christ. But the greatest among you shall be your servant."

I don't believe Jesus was saying that we shouldn't identify spiritual fathers, mothers, teachers, leaders, or mentors in our life, but rather, we are to make sure we are not looking to human beings—no matter how anointed they might be—to give us what we need for our spiritual growth. The anointing we see on others comes from God, and we are to honor those who have blessed us as well as acknowledge the Lord who gave them the anointing.

God is calling for mature believers to spiritually parent those whom He highlights. In a day when there is much emphasis on the need for spiritual fathers, mothers, and mentors, we need to ensure that we are not putting our trust in the arm of flesh. Let us love, honor, and appreciate—but not idolize—spiritual parents, for God alone is the author of His divine parental nature that flows through others into our lives.

As spiritual parents, let us learn from the Spirit of God how to lovingly turn our hearts to the next generation for His glory. In the same way, as spiritual children, let us learn from the Spirit how to respectfully discern and turn our hearts to those He marks as spiritual parents in our lives.

What Is a Spiritual Father or Mother, and What Is Their Responsibility?

A spiritual father or mother differs from a mentor (which we will cover later in this book) in that they walk in an anointing that manifests God's paternal and maternal nature. At times, as proximity and direction from the Spirit permit, they will come alongside a younger believer in the faith to cover, protect, nurture, and encourage them in their spiritual journey and ministry. They are not simply mentors in a specific skill or endowment as there is often a degree of nurture and covering involved.

A spiritual father or mother walks in an anointing that manifests God's paternal and maternal nature to cover, protect, nurture, and encourage a young believer in their spiritual journey or ministry.

For example, if you lead someone to Christ and disciple them in their faith with a deep love for them, you could be regarded as a spiritual parent. We see this in the life of the Apostle Paul. While in prison, he led Onesimus to the Lord and discipled him in his faith and ministry.

Philemon 1:10-16 (NIV)

That I appeal to you for my son Onesimus who became my son while I was in chains. Formerly he was useless to you, but now he has become useful both to you and to me. I am sending him—who is my very heart—back to you. I would have liked to keep him with me so that he could take your place in helping me while I am in chains for the gospel. But I did not want to do anything without your consent, so that any favor you do would not seem forced but would be voluntary. Perhaps the reason he was separated from you for a little while was that you might have him back forever—no longer as a slave, but better than a slave, as a dear brother. He is very dear to me but even dearer to you, both as a fellow man and as a brother in the Lord.

The Apostle Paul also refers to Timothy as his spiritual son in 1 Timothy 1:2, "To Timothy my true son in the faith…" In Acts 16:1-3, however, it is clear that Paul first met Timothy at Lystra, where Timothy is called "a disciple." Timothy was already saved, so it is not likely that Paul led Timothy to the Lord. It is more likely that Timothy's godly mother, Eunice, or grandmother, Lois, led him to the Lord when he was younger (2 Timothy 1:5). It appears that Paul served Timothy as an apostolic spiritual father as he watched over, nurtured, taught, covered, and encouraged Timothy's spiritual and ministry development. As an apostolic spiritual father, Paul appears to be the one Timothy was accountable to in his church. Paul loved and cared for him as a son, and Timothy respected and honored him as a father.

Elisha referred to Elijah as his father (2 Kings 2:12). He was farming when Elijah called him to follow. After leaving his family and assets, he served Elijah diligently. They shared life together as Elisha faithfully served and walked alongside Elijah. They had a solid bond, and Elisha became Elijah's successor.

Is It Vital to Have a Spiritual Parent other than God in Your Life?

David lacked healthy and authentic natural and spiritual parents in his life, but he did not lack being parented because he had the best parent of all, God Himself. He openly shared, "For my father and my mother have forsaken me, but the LORD will take me up. Teach me Your way, O LORD, and lead me in a level path (Psalm 27:10–11).

I cannot identify any one individual I would call my "spiritual father or mother." However, I was wonderfully parented by the Lord Himself, and I honestly have never felt that I missed having a spiritual father and mother in my life—back in the day, it wasn't even heard of much, so it wasn't an expectation.

Perhaps you are reading this book and think you are experiencing a deficit because you cannot identify a committed spiritual parent in your life. If so, I want to encourage you—Holy Spirit is with you and will give you everything you need, and He will be all things to you. The Holy Spirit used many people to acquaint me with the heart and ways of my Heavenly Father through public meetings, books, audio teachings, videos, interviews, and other resources.

I feel very well parented because the Lord took me up! It is possible to identify the Lord parenting you through various people, including many whom you might never meet. You can receive the impact of Father's heart through a passage in a book that touches you, listening to a teacher, or attending a seminar or conference.

When David said in Psalm 27:10 that his father and mother forsook him, but the Lord would take him up, he truly understood God's faithfulness as a spiritual Father and Mother through what he experienced in his life. God will do the same for you.

That being said, we can't ignore the solid prophetic voice of the Lord in this day where He is calling for His divine model to emerge: the hearts of the fathers (parents) turning to the children and the children to fathers (parents).

Malachi 4:5–6 (KJV)

Behold, I will send you Elijah the prophet before the coming of the great and dreadful day of the Lord:

And he shall turn the heart of the fathers to the children, and the heart of the children to their fathers, lest I come and smite the earth with a curse.

For the sake of definition, I refer to "fathers" as spiritual fathers *and* mothers and "children" as the next generation(s) of believers and leaders.

I personally have never asked anyone if I could be their spiritual mother, but I have many who call me this. Every time I hear someone call me their spiritual mother, I am humbled, and my spirit is once again awakened with the responsibility of such a call and privilege to serve. I have been on a journey for the last number of years, exploring the responsibilities of mothering spiritually and the available grace to fulfill such an assignment. It is not something to be taken lightly but with reverence and sobriety.

A Variety of Commitment Levels

I have discovered that there are various commitment levels as a spiritual parent. There are those whom I have trained and nurtured in ministry through close relationships and working together over the years. It has been my delight to observe their personal spiritual and ministry development, submit input, celebrate their successes, initiate disciplinary grace, and give support in times of disappointment and failure.

In these situations, there is an ongoing relationship between us that is nurtured and stewarded. I have worked closely with many of these individuals (and still do). The commitment I feel in my heart to them is very similar to what I feel with my own natural children. I love them as my own, and they know I am there for them, any time and in any way. We do life together, and I am often their primary covering and leader or at least a significant official advisor and covering. Some of them do not live near me, but we are in the relationship through phone, text, emails, and social media.

There are yet others whom I know more casually and have less involvement in their lives and ministries. I have, however, identified a maternal love and anointing that comes from God for them. I am aware when that anointing is present and functioning. I never lose sight that God Himself is the true and ultimate parent, but I recognize when He flows through me in this way. I know His deep love for those He calls me to serve.

I am a leader at our church and oversee and pastor an online congregation as well as cover a network of women in ministry. Even though I do not know each one personally or meet with them regularly, I feel a deep "mother-love" that the Father has deposited in me for those in the church and network.

The pastoral gift is very full of a father's (or mother's) love for the flock. Pastors are there for their members when they are in crisis, during their spiritual growth and development, when they get married, have children, and when they need help in their older years. Many congregation members will come to know their pastor as their primary spiritual father or mother.

There are also those I have never met who testify that my maternal anointing blesses them. Often when I am preparing a message or ministering to unseen crowds over media, I can feel the release of God's maternal anointing activated as I speak. I become upfront, personal, and filled with a mother's love for them, even though I am not relationally connected. It is by the Spirit, and I feel His love like a mother feels for her children. Sometimes I am introduced as a "mother in the faith." Their acknowledgment is due to this anointing.

In an hour where media gives us access to many ministries, messages, and events, many can identify someone they've never met as a spiritual parent. I have hosted media for many years both on global television networks and social media portals. Several years ago, I arrived in Sri Lanka for a ministry engagement. It was my very first time in the nation. As I was picking up my luggage, I heard a young man yell out, "Patricia King! Patricia King!" I turned to see him running toward me from the other side of the baggage claim, continuing to call my name. When he approached me, he gave me a big hug and said repeatedly, "You are my spiritual mother!" I was somewhat shocked as I had never met this young man before.

He explained to me that as a new believer, he had found me on television and watched all my programs; he had also devoured my teachings on other social media networks for several years. He said emphatically, "You are my spiritual mother." He felt the maternal anointing of God touch his heart through me, even though I had never met him or had contact with him until that day.

Turning Our Hearts to the Next Generation

According to our key scripture in Malachi 4:5-6 (cited above), we, as fathers and mothers in faith, must turn our hearts to the next generation for all to continue to live in blessing and not curse. I believe the emphasis in this passage should be on the word "hearts." If we turn our hearts toward the next generation in love and faith, the father and mother anointing of God will be activated. And if the next generation turns their hearts toward the older generation, honor and love will be activated.

SPIRITUAL FATHERS AND MOTHERS, ARISE

A friend of mine, who is a Generation X[1] leader, found herself filled with love for Generation Z.[2] Before long, the Lord was using her powerfully through social media to reach thousands in that generation. She identified a mother's heart in the spirit and was able to sow greatly into those who connected with her. Most of those she ministered to never connected with her in person, but God's maternal anointing touched their lives through her social media outlet because her heart was turned toward them.

I was watching a young minister online as he shared an inspiring, faith-building, and character-aligning message in an auditorium that was filled with well over ten thousand of the younger generation. He was in his early thirties while his audience was mainly between 14 years of age to mid-20s. I was greatly impressed with not only the content and delivery of his message, but with the heart of "fatherly love" he carried for those he was ministering to. His heart came through as loud and clear as his message. His audience was fully connected to him and engaged in his message. It was beautiful to see. I am convinced that many in the audience were touched by Father's heart through his ministry.

A spiritual parent, no matter what age, turns their heart to those they are serving, but the ways in which they engage will be varied. Some will be very one-on-one and personal while others will not.

I believe Holy Spirit will lead specifically and uniquely in every given scenario. We often want to know the rules of

---

1 The generation born after Baby Boomers. Generation X born between 1965 and 1980.
2 The generation born after the Millennials. Generation Z born between 1997 and 2012.

engagement rather than the One who is the giver of all wisdom, counsel, insight, and instruction. For example, your responsibilities will differ depending on what level of commitment and covenant relationship you have with those you are spiritually parenting. Holy Spirit will guide you in each situation and the ways for one might not work for another.

There are two foundational keys to regard as we arise as spiritual fathers and mothers:

1. We have hearts that turn with authentic love to serve the next generation's well-being and calling.
2. We acknowledge that God alone is the progenitor who imparts His paternal and maternal love that enables us to lay down our lives and support those He invites us to serve. Even though we carry and model His heart, we turn the attention of those we serve to acknowledge and worship Him as the true Father (Mother).

What Is Holding You Back?

The prophetic word for fathers to turn their hearts to the children and the children to the fathers is not an option. God is looking for your "yes," and when you give Him your yes, He will anoint you for the assignment and grant you everything you need. It is easy to hold on to things that hold you back like, "I don't feel adequate, I don't have the time, or I don't have the desire," but God can give you everything you are lacking. He can fill inadequacy, create the time, and load you with desire.

Others are held back because they have not had good models of spiritual parents in their lives. Some have even had abusive

> The prophetic word for fathers to turn their hearts to the children and the children to the fathers is not an option. God is looking for your "yes."

and controlling spiritual parents, leaving them wounded. It is important to receive healing for these wounds. God cares about your soul. I think of David who did not have healthy parenting. He was overlooked, neglected, and used by his natural father, and his spiritually anointed and appointed leader (Saul) was abusive toward him, even attempting to kill him.

Despite these hardships, David remained strong and became a powerful king who is celebrated to this day. When you read the Psalms he wrote, you can see him drawing what he needed for a healthy soul from the Lord. We do need to forgive our natural and spiritual parents for their failures in order to be free ourselves. The pain we experienced in the past does not define our future and neither does it define us.

You must deal with your woundedness, as unhealed areas can trigger harmful behaviors and choices that can hurt others. Receive from the Lord the healing you need, and then you can give Him your yes (more on this topic in another chapter).

Some do not believe they are qualified to be spiritual parents because they have failed in natural parenting. This is understandable, but we can always learn from our mistakes if we are humble and willing to take responsibility. You can be forgiven for your failures and learn new parenting skills from the Lord. It is important that you correct the wrongs and receive the best of what He has to give you.

If you feel that there are factors holding you back, you simply need to ask and be willing to receive. It all begins with your willingness. Sometimes we need to pray, "Lord I am unwilling, but make me willing." He will give you everything you need to be whole, blessed, and qualified.

When you give Him your yes, you will not need to go out looking for spiritual children to parent or places to offer your services. The Lord will honor your yes and then orchestrate the connections and grant you the wisdom you need. The connections will not be forced but by grace will be "supernaturally natural."

Some of you are not ready to be spiritual parents as you are still young in the Lord. You are called to identify and honor spiritual parents (this is covered in later chapters). But many of you are ready now. Are you willing to receive God's paternal or maternal anointing for the next generation? If you give Him your yes, you will become part of His plan. He has need of you.

CONVERSATION POINT

Discuss what it means and what it looks like for us to turn our hearts as fathers/mothers to the next generation.

ACTIVATION

1. Identify anything that is holding you back from giving God your yes, and ask Him to make you willing.
2. Have you recognized an area that needs healing in your life? If so, make a quality decision to get the help you need.
3. Officially give God your yes.

Chapter Three

FIVE KEY ATTRIBUTES OF SPIRITUAL PARENTS
Patricia King

Whether you are looking to identify spiritual parents in your life, preparing to be a spiritual parent or both, you will be interested in reviewing the five critical attributes of a spiritual parent. I share more from a maternal perspective, but I believe the following attributes are characteristics our Father in heaven is looking for in the lives of all those who will represent His parenting heart for the coming generation(s).

1. The Attribute of Faithfulness in Prayer, Intercession, and Warfare

One of the most powerful ways to turn your heart toward those you spiritually parent is through prayer. While in prayer, you can quickly feel and sense the Lord's love and passion for them. Prayer is where you can receive His nature and perspective for them.

Your intercession will bless those whom the Lord calls you to serve as a spiritual parent. God answers prayer, and the covering love you offer them as one who stands in the gap is significant.

I have a list of those I pray for in my office. I regularly decree blessings over their lives, and God honors it. I have discovered that as I pray, the Lord will bring specific individuals to my heart and grants me more detail as I wait on Him. Sometimes I will receive specific encouragement in prayer that I can send to them or an alert to check in to see how they are doing.

We all face warfare in our journey and require some "extra forces" to help in the battle. Spiritual parents have often endured similar attacks and can give wisdom amid the struggle. They offer their overcoming faith to support their spiritual children in battle.

Those I have built relationships with know they can text me and request prayer or connection anytime.

When your heart is turned to the next generation, you will find yourself praying general prayers for their steadfastness in faith, values, and truth. You might never meet them in person, but your prayers will offer the opportunity for God to touch their lives and ministries. As you pray for the next generation, your love and commitment to them will increase.

I often feel the rising of what I refer to as a "mother-bear" passion when I sense danger for the Body of Christ and specifically for the next generation. It is a deep desire to protect them and keep them safe from deception and harmful ways. As I pray, the Lord will often inspire a message or deliver a prophetic exhortation from His heart that will help them come into His safe covering and shelter.

2. The Attribute of Godliness

I conversed with a young man as he shared his journey into ministry. He revealed how his spiritual father and mentor had been exposed publicly as a drunkard, womanizer, sex addict, abuser, deceiver, and a poor steward of ministry finances. This young man's heart was broken, and he felt deeply betrayed, not only concerning the ungodly actions of his "spiritual father" but also his refusal to repent and take ownership of the multiple confirmed allegations. This young man was crushed, not knowing how to move forward. His spiritual father was very anointed and had a winning, charismatic personality. How could he manifest so much of God's presence yet live in so much darkness?

This young minister admitted that he had witnessed behaviors in his spiritual father's life that crossed moral lines, but for a long time he had shrugged it off as something that needed to be covered by love and grace—after all, his leader was so anointed. Unfortunately, others were under this spiritual leader's covering that followed his example. Spiritual parents are responsible for modeling righteous and godly behavior or it will affect many adversely.

As the founder of Voice4Victims (a ministry that gives support to those who have been abused sexually, emotionally, spiritually, or financially in the church), I hear of too many stories of leaders and spiritual "parents" who have modeled ungodly behaviors.

Paul encourages believers to follow him as he follows the Lord.

> "Follow my example, as I follow the example of Christ."
> – *1 Corinthians 11:1* (NIV)

Paul had confidence that if believers followed him as he followed the Lord, they would not falter. Are you living in a godly manner? Are people safe to follow you? I often encourage those I am leading to live their lives in a way that if a child were to mirror or follow everything they said or did, they would never stumble.

If you are going to be a spiritual father or mother to the next generation(s), you cannot live carelessly, giving in to fleshly indulgences or the love of the world and its lusts. As spiritual parents, we must partake of God's divine nature and model it well without double standards. Raise the bar high and live blameless before God and man.

The church and the world desperately need godly examples today. We see rebellion, dishonor, lawlessness, immorality, faithlessness, and offense in society. What if in this current generation, we see the emergence of radical believers who are obedient, honoring, lawful, moral, faith-empowered, and unoffendable because they've had spiritual parents who model and teach these Kingdom values? I long for this. Let's create it!

3. The Attribute of Selfless Love and Care

Motives of the heart are everything! Love always desires the highest good for the sake of another and is not motivated by selfish gain. The spiritual fathers and mothers God is raising up in this hour are those who embrace the cross—death to selfish ambition and motives. They give themselves to the next generation because they love them!

Motives of the heart are everything! Love always desires the highest good for the sake of another and is not motivated by selfish gain.

It is easy to say, "I love you" but often challenging to walk it out. Your love will be tested repeatedly. In a natural family, you will sometimes find one of the children more challenging than the others. They try your patience, and sometimes you might wonder if they will develop well. In observing these family dynamics over the years, often the most trying child is the one that accomplishes the most in their adult years. It's interesting to watch. As a spiritual parent, you need "love eyes" to see beyond the "stone in the rough."

Some of my most fruitful, successful, and beloved children in the faith required me to see them through God's love potential in their early journeys. Some of them had so many visible rough edges that I often had other believers and friends give me warnings about my involvement with them because they "discerned" their challenging issues. God will help you see way beyond those things—and you will need to if you are going to love well.

All things are possible with God. I often see spiritual children like flowers with all their potential beauty in bud form. I remember an outstanding rose bush that was given to us as a gift years ago. It was a thorny group of brown stems in a pot of dirt when we received it from a friend. It didn't look like much, but we reluctantly planted it in the garden.

Although it initially looked without promise, it had hidden potential that would eventually shock us. The bush grew tender leaves, and small, closed buds became visible. The plant grew over time, and the buds emerged with their own glory. As they opened, they offered a great surprise. I will never forget the first rose that fully opened. It boasted multiple colors and shades of light coral, yellow, pink, and orange. It smelled like sweet peaches and was massive in size—about the size of a grapefruit! Then, one after another, we saw the entire bush come alive with beauty. That rose bush produced the most beautiful flowers every year following. Many were elated when they gazed upon that bush and its blooms and smelled its fragrance. What began as a pot of dirt, sticks, and thorns was transformed into something of great value that blessed many. All that beauty was hidden in the original pot. I would never have guessed at first glance what the full potential was.

There is so much potential in each precious life God brings to us, and as spiritual fathers and mothers, we can both see and nurture that potential. I believe that Jesus modeled this when He chose His twelve disciples. They were all rough and unpolished, but they transformed the world. Jesus saw their potential!

Another aspect of love is caring for spiritual children when they experience hurt and disappointment. Life is full of painful moments and circumstances, and sometimes spiritual children will need a generous dose of reassurance ... and a big hug! As a spiritual parent, you are not required to "fix" the problem unless it is wise to do so and you are able, but rather to help your spiritual children know how to lean on the Lord as they walk through their dark and overwhelming moments. When you are there alongside them, it gives them strength. You might need to give up some time, sleep, and some comfort of your own, but that is what selfless love looks like.

When you choose to love, you will bond with your spiritual children and know how to care for and nurture them in their time of need. We always want to encourage them to be bold, confident, and courageous, and to avoid co-dependency, but there are times when they will need extra reassurance.

Like natural parenting, spiritual parenting is an honor and privilege but also requires sacrifice. You would never use your spiritual children to give yourself an advantage, but like Jesus, you lay your life down for them, serving them well. When you love them beautifully and fully, they will one day rise and bless you because of the seed selflessly sown into them by you.

4. The Attribute of Loving Discipline

The writer of Hebrews reveals the importance of discipline for every believer. It will help us grow strong in faith and character.

Hebrews 12:4-11 (NASB 1995)

You have not yet resisted to the point of shedding blood in your striving against sin; and you have forgotten the exhortation which is addressed to you as sons, "MY SON, DO NOT REGARD LIGHTLY THE DISCIPLINE OF THE LORD, NOR FAINT WHEN YOU ARE REPROVED BY HIM; FOR THOSE WHOM THE LORD LOVES HE DISCIPLINES, AND HE SCOURGES EVERY SON WHOM HE RECEIVES."

It is for discipline that you endure; God deals with you as with sons; for what son is there whom his father does not discipline? But if you are without discipline, of which all have become partakers, then you are illegitimate children and not sons. Furthermore, we had earthly fathers to discipline us, and we respected them; shall we not much rather be subject to the Father of spirits, and live? For they disciplined us for a short time as seemed best to them, but He disciplines us for our good, so that we may share His holiness. All discipline for the moment seems not to be joyful, but sorrowful; yet to those who have been trained by it, afterwards it yields the peaceful fruit of righteousness.

A spiritual father or mother might need to help those they are caring for by speaking the truth in love. If we genuinely discipline from God's heart, it will be to serve them well and not because we are frustrated or upset. We want everyone we serve to grow strong and secure in the Lord.

Discipline usually involves confrontation, which is never a pleasant task but can produce lasting fruit when received well. When confronting or calling for alignment, do so with grace.

We see Peter as a great apostle of the early church, but he endured a great deal of course correction in his journey as a disciple of the Lord. In his epistles, he speaks of the power of endurance and the fruit that it brings. He was speaking from experience! Jesus did not let him remain in behaviors that were incompatible with his godly call to sonship and apostleship.

Eli and His Sons

The failure to bring correction and discipline as a spiritual parent can be fatal. We see this in the life of Eli and his sons (1 Samuel 2:12-25). Eli was the leader, a devoted high priest of the Lord's house. His two sons, also priests under his leadership, were involved in many transgressions (immorality, extortion, abusive control, and misuse of position). Eli was very aware of this and had even addressed the issue with them but unfortunately never enforced correction or discipline. He allowed these behaviors and transgressions to continue under his leadership without restraint. As a result, both his sons died in battle, the ark of the covenant was taken by the Philistines, and Eli died following. The manifest glory of God departed from Israel (1 Samuel 4:1-21).

What you fail to confront, you condone and will be held accountable.

5. The Attribute of Generosity

Sow into your spiritual children and the next generation extravagantly and intentionally. You have probably heard the phrase, "Our ceiling is the floor of the next generation." This is regarding the building of a legacy. What do you possess that can be sown into the next generation?

Recently, I have enjoyed reflecting on all the Lord has taught me over the decades I have known and served Him. I've realized that there were many things I took for granted. A nugget of revealed wisdom or truth can quickly become so normalized in your life that you fail to realize many have never been introduced to those things. I've intentionally prepared teachings and hosted online mentorship groups to share some of these nuggets, insights, and revelations. I want to sow the wisdom that the Lord has so richly granted me into the next generation deliberately and generously.

Another area the Lord has been speaking to me about is to sow my time generously. Often in a day, I will be on the phone or texting with those I love and nurture, or I will spend time in prayers and decrees for them.

As a spiritual parent, you will find times when one of your precious children is going through a very painful season or needs counsel regarding the direction they are seeking. This is an opportunity to sow heartfelt attention and ministry into their lives. Engagement with one another builds bonds, but it takes time and availability.

Investing time into the dreams and assignments of your spiritual children is also an honor. I love running alongside them as their cheering squad when they forge their trails into new frontiers. When you do this, you build memories, and this is important and enriching. Jesus modeled "doing life" with His disciples. They ministered together, ate together, and traveled together. They bonded as He gave them His time, and much of the rich and profound input and impartation took place, "as they went."

We desire our spiritual children to cultivate and steward their own precious journey with the Lord and utilize their faith to fulfill God's purposes, but we must also be sensitive to what

> **We desire our spiritual children to cultivate and steward their own precious journey with the Lord ... but we must also be sensitive to what they require from us along the way.**

they require from us along the way. It is an honor to give and to bless.

As parents of natural children, we provide for their needs such as food, clothing, and shelter, but we teach them as they grow to exercise their abilities to produce from their own initiative as part of training them to stir their potential to prosper and see dreams and goals fulfilled.

I remember my oldest son at age 11, sharing how much he wanted a computer when they first came on the market decades ago. My husband and I did not have the means to purchase it for him then, but I said, "You can surely have your dream come true. You can work on your paper route, save your money, and buy one. God will help you, and we will be in your cheering section!" We generously shared wisdom with him on defining his dream, setting goals, working hard, and stewarding what came into his hand. This was what we had to give in that season.

We added financially what we could from time to time, but for the most part, he raised the bulk of the money on his own. After several months, his dream came true. He worked hard to make money to purchase it. He saved every penny and sacrificed other things to achieve his dream. If we had bought the computer for him, he never would have experienced the faith journey he walked, the lessons he learned, or the fulfillment he felt. Over the years, the Lord blessed him greatly. At the time of this writing, he is in his late forties, a hard worker, a good steward of resources, and has been blessed with bounty.

As spiritual parents, it is an honor to sow resources and finances into our spiritual children as the Lord leads and at the right timing. We have joyfully invested much into the next generation, but we do so strategically and with wisdom so that they also flex their faith muscles. Their roots will become strong as they persevere in their faith and overcome obstacles. Resistance training is important for building muscle. No resistance, no growth. As a spiritual parent, don't jump in right away to meet every need, but allow your spiritual sons and daughters to experience the joy of the breakthrough into greater realms of faith and strength. Partnering with next-generation believers as they walk out their destiny is a rich blessing.

Our Father in heaven is an extravagant giver. He gave His very own Son for all. There is no good or beneficial thing that He withheld from us. This generous nature is in us as believers, and we are to bless our spiritual children with the riches He has bestowed on us.

There are so many other attributes that we could study and embrace, but these are the five I have found to be the greatest core values for serving the next generation as a spiritual mother or father.

CONVERSATION POINT

Discuss the possible impact you see for the next generation if spiritual parents emerge, manifesting the attributes discussed in this chapter.

ACTIVATION

Have you identified those whom the Lord has raised up to manifest His parental nature in your life? Make a list, and next to their names, write a paragraph on how they have shown you the Father or Mother heart of God … and then, send them a thank you note or gift of appreciation.

Chapter Four

AVOIDING CODEPENDENCE AND GUILT TRIPS
Patricia King

Avoiding Codependency

I have seen some tragic cases of codependency take place between spiritual parents and spiritual children. Codependency is often defined as a "relationship addiction." One of the greatest factors in remaining free and safe from codependency is to establish your trust in God as your primary giver of everything you need. As we have already shared, God has first place in everything and is the source and supply of all we need. When He has first place in our hearts, then it is next to impossible to become addicted to a relationship.

Addiction involves a chemical reaction in the brain when an individual reacts to a substance that can give a surge of joy, elation, emotional fulfillment, deep peace, extreme satisfaction, and ecstasy. An individual can be addicted to food, alcohol, drugs, sexual stimulation, exercise, work, and people, to name a few examples.

The reward and stress systems are two primary brain circuits engaged in triggering addiction. The reward system provides pleasurable feelings when you experience enjoyable activities such as eating a great dessert or the rush you get after a fulfilling workout at the gym. On the other hand, the stress system of the brain provides signals that help you amid threats, crisis situations, or dangers.

The reward system releases dopamine, which is a chemical that makes you feel happiness, love, and pleasure. The stress system in the brain alerts the adrenals to release cortisol which creates an increase in your heart rate and blood pressure and causes you to feel "super-strength." It produces your natural "flight or fight" response.

When these two systems are triggered at the same time, it is a setup for addiction. For example, let's say an individual is internally stressed because they have been feeling rejected, lonely, and depressed. The stress system of the brain will be activated.

If they then were to connect with someone who makes them feel safe, accepted, valued, and extremely loved, they will feel good, happy, and strengthened because the brain has signaled the release of chemicals from both systems. The body is dispatching both dopamine and cortisol at the same time. After spending time with this person, they feel joyful pleasure, hope, a sense of well-being, and exhilaration. The brain has created neuropathways to facilitate the feelings and responses. When the feelings wear down, the brain craves more of that feeling. As a result, the individual desires to see them again, and as dependency increases, they could find themselves creating opportunities to be with them or connect in some way. In co-dependency, you must have more of them—you need them.

The other person could then unknowingly feed the trigger and increase the addiction. They might also begin to feel some pleasure from being so needed. The emotions are now connecting, and both individuals want to be with each other more and more and at a deeper and deeper level.

This is codependency. As with any addiction, in the beginning stages, it does not appear to be troublesome, but eventually, the substance will cause you to crash and burn. The co-dependent relationship usually becomes painful and unmanageable over time, but due to the addiction, the brain remembers the first jolt of ecstasy and is determined to find it again.

A very sad situation, years ago, portrays this addiction. A woman (whom I will call Linda) was very broken and feeling unloved in her marriage. She had suffered abuse as a child and youth and then got married at nineteen with a child on the way. Her brokenness was never healed, and she developed a need to be needed. She was a very loving, compassionate, and tender person.

A young teenage girl (whom I will call Sara), who had lived homeless on the streets for a couple of years, came to the Lord, and Linda and her husband took her in. They were struggling in their marriage, and Linda longed for purpose in her life. She felt compassion for Sara. Sara was deeply broken and desperately needed the love a mother could give. This was a perfect setup for disaster.

Linda took on the role of her spiritual mother, and it wasn't long before things went south. Linda initially ministered to Sara under a pure anointing, and Sara felt the love, power, and pleasure that Linda's ministry offered for the first time in her life. She needed and wanted more. Linda felt needed and rewarded. They were compelled to be with each other more and more and became deceptively codependent, believing that the Lord had ordained the relationship. They were entwined emotionally and became extremely co-dependent. Unfortunately, the story did not end well. It crossed lines into sexual immorality. Linda and her husband lost their marriage, and their children suffered greatly. Linda and Sara lived as a couple for a season until eventually, their relationship fell apart. Sara left, and Linda was devastated, alone, and deeply wounded. I have unfortunately seen this happen more than once.

In another situation, a teenager (I will name Bradley) was involved in a youth group at church. He had grown up without a father or strong male figure in his life. His youth leader (I will name Terry) was in his twenties and greatly encouraged him. Bradley felt fatherly attributes from Terry, who took Bradley under his wing. Terry spent time with Bradley, helping him with his studies, treating him to a meal once in a while, attending his sports games at school, and processing some stressful moments in Bradley's life on a heart-to-heart level with him.

Bradley began to demand Terry's time and attention constantly. Terry tried to pull back, which made Bradley press in even more as he feared losing the relationship. Eventually, Terry had to draw some boundaries, leaving Bradley confused and devastated.

Terry had filled the emotional gap Bradley received from growing up fatherless, but Bradley became addicted to Terry's love, care, and attention.

Acknowledging God alone as the One who meets all our needs will keep us safe from relational addiction and inordinate affection. If we take this stand, we will not then "need" someone to fill the void—He does. He is to be acknowledged as the One we lean on and the One whom we receive from first. Then, when He brings people into our life to represent Him, we appreciate and enjoy them as His gift to us, but we are not dependent on them because our heart belongs to Him. We are less likely to cross emotional lines. Everything and everyone in our life is to be under His wonderful, kind, and loving Lordship.

Some might wonder, "How do I put Him first?" Some struggle because they cannot feel, see, or touch Him. God is invisible, but He is very real! The Bible teaches that the "righteous shall live by faith" (see Romans 1:17; Galatians 3:11; Hebrews 10:38; Habakkuk 2:4). Hebrews 11:6 teaches us that when we approach God, it must be by faith and that we must "believe that He is," and that "He is a rewarder of those who diligently seek Him."

The following points might help bring understanding and instruction on how to position yourself before God to receive from Him.

What will keep us safe from relational addiction and inordinate affection is acknowledging God alone as the One who meets all our needs.

---

1. Believe that He is present whether you feel Him or not. He is there. He is real. He is in love with you—He is for you (Hebrews 11:6a).

2. Give Him your heart. Proclaim in His presence that He is your first love. He is your Lord (owner and master of all you are and all you have), your Savior, your King, your Father, Mother, Friend, Provider, Counselor, and more.

3. As you speak this out in His presence, you might not feel you are connecting. You might not sense His nearness—but believe He is there and speak from your heart. Yield to Him completely. Trust Him with your life—every aspect of it.

    If you are not sure that you are able to surrender all to Him fully, but you want to, then let Him know that, and ask for His help. Perhaps pray something like this: "Lord, I want to fully surrender my heart to You, but I don't know if I can. Increase Your grace in my life, and enable me to trust and yield my all to You. Grant me my desire. Help me."

4. Acknowledge the specific need in your life. Before going to anyone else, through faith, approach Him and declare that you trust Him to meet your longing. By faith, receive Him into that area of your life. Notice that in Mark 11:24, Jesus teaches that it is WHEN you pray that you RECEIVE (by faith) and not when there is an outward sign. The moment you receive your need as met (by faith), you have it. The manifestation will follow. "Therefore I say to you, whatever things you ask when you pray, believe that you receive *them*, and you will have *them*."

5. Thank Him and praise Him with gratitude for fulfilling you and meeting your need (even if you don't feel or sense a

change). By faith, drink of His goodness and receive His rich love into your area of need. Don't rush this process. Remain in His presence until, through your faith, you have secured the reality in your heart that He is who fulfills this area of your life.

6. Worship Him as your ONE who meets your every need. "And my God shall supply all your need according to His riches in glory by Christ Jesus" (Philippians 4:19). Worship Him as your ONE even before there is any outward sign of fulfillment.

7. Following this time, He will orchestrate what you need and bring forth provision (people, material substance, circumstances, etc.). Sometimes, He will bring a person into your life to help you, make you aware of resources, or manifest a miracle, but He will lead the journey as you follow. When you recognize His provision, thank Him, and acknowledge in your heart that the blessing came from Him. "Every good gift and every perfect gift is from above, and comes down from the Father of lights, with whom there is no variation or shadow of turning" (James 1:17).

8. Continue to depend on Him, and give Him first place in all things.

Parental Guilt

Parents often feel guilty when they see their children grow to make tragic and destructive choices in their lives. They believe they failed as parents. When you become a natural parent, you have no training. You suddenly become fully responsible for the infant you are holding in your arms, and every season of development in your child's life offers you an uncharted territory to explore. Some of your parenting skills will be exemplary while others might be far from perfect or in some cases, missing altogether. As natural parents, we all need grace as we attempt to do our best for our children. Even though the Spirit will convict you when necessary, He does not want you to carry guilt and shame. You repent when convicted and receive His forgiveness. When appropriate, it is important to ask your child to forgive you.

It is the same in spiritual parenting. You will possibly make mistakes, but God does not want you to be weighed down with accusation.

I have seen children raised in horrible circumstances. Their parents were neglectful and abusive, yet the children grew to make right choices and enjoyed a full and wonderful life. They were assets to their community and to those who were in relationship with them.

On the other hand, I have seen children raised in perfect environments with loving and caring parents who grew up rebellious, living lives bound by addiction or steeped in crime.

Bad things happen to good people, but everyone makes their own decisions in life. Whether you were blessed with loving parents or abusive ones, you make your choice as to how you walk through life. You are responsible.

This is the same with spiritual parents and children. Everyone makes their own choices and decisions. Healthy spiritual parenting helps tremendously, but it is not a guarantee that spiritual children will make the right choices. I am grateful and blessed to have many wonderful spiritual children who are stellar individuals living godly lives and bringing light to their world. Sadly, I have a few who have made poor or destructive choices for their lives and who have hurt others as a result. Who is responsible for their choices? They are. Hopefully, in time, they will turn. I never stop loving or praying for them, but they are the ones who will live with their choices. I am not responsible, and I am to bear no guilt or accusation for their choices, and neither are you. As spiritual parents, we are to acknowledge our mistakes and shortcomings in all humility and learn vital lessons, but we must not be self-condemned or clothed in oppressive guilt and shame. We receive forgiveness from the Lord and pray for His grace to cover any mistakes. We humbly make amends wherever needed and possible and move forward into maturity.

You Are Not Alone

In the business world, the son or daughter of an influencer who owns a large corporation will gain privileges that they never earned. They will often be put in key positions in the company, not because they are best suited or qualified, but because they are the child of the owner. At times, those sons or daughters bring harm to the integrity and growth of the company as they do not rightly represent their parents. They were given privilege and resource, but they made wrong choices.

> **As spiritual parents, we are to acknowledge our mistakes and shortcomings in all humility and learn vital lessons, but we must not be self-condemned or clothed in oppressive guilt and shame.**

It is the same for us in the church. Just because you, as an anointed leader, have a cherished relationship with a spiritual son or daughter, there is no guarantee that they will represent you or the Lord well. We find examples of this in the Bible.

God declared that David was a man after His own heart (Acts 13:22). Although not perfect, David was an excellent king and followed the Lord with all his soul. His son Absalom, however, did not follow in his father's footsteps but rebelled and even attempted to steal his father's throne.

Samuel, although a godly man, was succeeded by his two sons who were appointed priests, but they were corrupt and vile in their ways.

Jesus had twelve close disciples who shared life with Him daily for over three years. He was a perfect leader and spiritual father, yet one of them betrayed Him and another denied Him.

God, Himself, is the perfect parent, yet His people rebelled. In Genesis 6, the Lord destroyed the earth by a flood because He regretted that He had ever made man. Ouch! That is a lot of parental pain. If God, the perfect parent, had children who made disappointing choices, then if you are in the same situation, you are not alone! He understands your pain.

As a spiritual parent, you want to do your very best through God's grace and anointing to give all you can to create inner strength, faith, and godly character in those you are called to. You want to be a good example for them so that if they follow your example, they will become better believers and ministers because of it.

As a spiritual parent, you are responsible for your choices. Choose wisely.

Your spiritual children are responsible for theirs. May they choose wisely too.

Ezekiel 18:4 (NASB 1995)

"Behold, all souls are Mine; the soul of the father as well as the soul of the son is Mine; the soul who sins shall die."

CONVERSATION POINT

Discuss the difference between taking responsibility for ungodly behaviors, while avoiding taking the responsibility of guilt for another's choices when your behaviors have influenced them.

ACTIVATION

Identify any areas of your life that you have blamed a parent or leader for your decisions. If Holy Spirit brings any situations to mind, repent for judgments you put on them and take responsibility for your choices.

Chapter Five

MENTORS AND LEADERS

Patricia King and Benjamin Deitrick

Mentors

Patricia King

God's ways are unsearchable and past finding out (Romans 11:33). This means your growth and progression in life are indeed a journey in which you will always have more to discover. You are invited to walk into new, uncharted territories with the Lord and learn more about Him in every season. What an awesome adventure! There is never boredom in a life committed to God. What you learn in one season will prepare you for the next.

In your spiritual journey, the Lord will give you mentors. A dictionary definition of mentor is:

(noun) an experienced and trusted adviser; (verb) advise or train someone, especially a younger colleague.[3]

In the fields of business, technology, sports, and media, a mentor offers instruction, coaching, advice, and modeling of a skill to those they are training and equipping.

Spiritual mentors are those who are seasoned, experienced, and mature in an area of spiritual life, skill, and ministry, and who are willing to model, teach, and impart their wisdom and specific endowments to others. Teachers are those who will give understanding on a subject. Mentors can be teachers, but they are also activators and work with those they are mentoring to see them skilled in their areas of training.

I have met many who had a deep-felt need for a mentor to walk with them in close relationship throughout their journey, but most believers have not had this type of personal connection offered to them. However, this does not mean that you cannot be well mentored.

Again, the answer to our longing is found in acknowledging the Lord. The Holy Spirit is ultimately your Mentor, and He is outstanding. Look at what Jesus says about the Holy Spirit's call to mentor you:

John 14:26 (NASB 1995)

But the Helper, the Holy Spirit, whom the Father will send in My name, He will teach you all things, and bring to your remembrance all that I said to you.

---

3 Oxford Online Dictionary

John 16:13-15 (NASB 1995)

But when He, the Spirit of truth, comes, He will guide you into all the truth; for He will not speak on His own initiative, but whatever He hears, He will speak; and He will disclose to you what is to come. He will glorify Me, for He will take of Mine and will disclose it to you. All things that the Father has are Mine; therefore I said that He takes of Mine and will disclose it to you.

Romans 8:14 (NASB 1995)

For all who are being led by the Spirit of God, these are sons of God.

1 John 2:27 (NASB 1995)

And as for you, the anointing which you received from Him remains in you, and you have no need for anyone to teach you; but as His anointing teaches you about all things, and is true and is not a lie, and just as it has taught you, you remain in Him.

When I was a new believer, I had friends who were ministering the gifts of the Holy Spirit. They were trained by Mary Goddard, an anointed minister in this field, and they highly recommended that I take a one-week course she was teaching on the subject. I experienced radical spiritual growth on many levels as she instructed on the nine gifts of the Spirit outlined in 1 Corinthians 12:1-10. She both instructed us from the Bible and enthusiastically activated us. It was life-transforming for me. I decided to take the course a second and third time so that

I could glean more on the subject. It wasn't only the content she taught under the anointing that empowered me; I was also deeply impacted by how she modeled the nature of Christ as she activated and encouraged us in the operation of the gifts with patience and love. Later I had the opportunity to travel with her on a few occasions and then eventually worked with/for her. She was a mentor to me and many in the gifts of the Spirit.

Mentorship usually involves instruction and guidance in one area of spiritual endowment or skill. I know those who have been mentored by evangelists in the ministry of soul winning, others who have been mentored by prophets in dreams, interpretation of dreams, prophetic gifts, words of knowledge, and the "seer" anointing, others who have been mentored by intercessory generals in prayer ministry, and still others who have received mentoring in leadership by seasoned and respected spiritual leaders. There is no end to the areas of spiritual life and ministry in which you can be mentored, and as believers, we should be eager to always grow in new understanding and skills.

As aforementioned, your ultimate Mentor is the Holy Spirit Himself, but He will appoint individuals whom He has prepared to serve you and help you grow and expand in skill and understanding.

When choosing a mentor, look for those who are anointed, mature, solid in character, and effective in their field of ministry. For example, you would not want someone to mentor you in financial growth if they are bound by poverty. You would not want someone instructing and coaching you in marriage if they have a failed marriage. In the same way, for spiritual mentoring,

> **Your ultimate Mentor is the Holy Spirit, but He will appoint individuals He has prepared to serve you and help you grow and expand in skill and understanding.**

you want to be instructed and coached by those who are fruitful and established in their field.

In my early spiritual development, I was blessed to be mentored by a great man of God, regarding living on the foundation of unwavering faith in God's Word.

I never met this man of God or even had a personal connection with him via phone, email, or other means of communication, but he was definitely a God-appointed mentor. I devoured his books, videos, teachings, and a few times even attended large rallies and meetings where he was ministering. Through his teaching sessions, he always encouraged activating the Word of God through unwavering faith.

The Holy Spirit used him powerfully to mentor me. Galatians 6:6 (AMP) teaches us that, "The one who is taught the word [of God] is to share all good things with his teacher [contributing to his spiritual and material support]." In response—as I have done with all those who have impacted me spiritually—I financially partnered with his ministry and prayed for him regularly.

Most of my "mentorships" in spiritual growth and ministry were seldom via relational "hands-on" coaching but rather through the Holy Spirit's leading to specific resources of ministers, during specific seasons, for specific training.

In your relationship with Holy Spirit, He will give you invitations to new areas of spiritual growth, skill, and maturity. As He calls you higher, He will also highlight individuals who will empower you in that season and area of growth. Some you might have personal relationship and connection with, but many of your mentors will likely be those who enhance your walk through their public ministries, training, resource, and online groups. Behind it all is your true Mentor, Holy Spirit.

Don't wait for a mentor to come to you when you can go to them. Identify your area of hunger and then find the help you need. Holy Spirit will direct you.

I have been part of a team who encourages the body of Christ to be seasoned as God's messengers. One area of training we offer is how to write a book, blog, or devotional. The team has very skilled and seasoned practitioners in various areas of writing, editing, and marketing. It is all online via an interactive platform where we inspire, teach, host question-and-answer sessions, and coach.

Those who train with us might never meet us in person, but they connect with us "face to face" on the online platform. They are writing books, blogs, and devotionals. Each of them saw the instruction being offered and then moved forward to sign up for the course. They didn't wait for someone to approach them and say, "I will be your personal trainer." They pursued the opportunity and were mentored to the degree that they made the investment of time, focus, and money. It was available to them, but they needed to move toward it and partake.

You can receive great teaching, instruction, and modeling, but if you do not apply it or exercise it, you will not grow. Mentors will not do the work for you, but they can show you the way. Your growth depends on your response, application, and practice, and not on the abilities or reputation of your mentor. You might have a seasoned mentor who is world-renowned, yet you will still not grow if you do not apply with diligence what you have been coached in. Sitting in a mentoring session doesn't create skill in you, in the same way as sitting in a restaurant doesn't make you a chef. Practice is required.

A coach at the gym might not be a father or mother to a child—but a great coach, nonetheless. Likewise, not all spiritual mentors are spiritual fathers or mothers. However, many are both. A spiritual mentor who teaches a skill might not carry the heart of a spiritual parent, but you will find those who carry both anointings.

Bishop Bill Hamon, for example, is known as one of the key apostolic fathers of the prophetic movement. He is truly a spiritual father to many leaders and believers in the prophetic movement and is rightly globally acknowledged as such. He is also an outstanding teacher, prophet, prolific author—and additionally, an anointed mentor. I remember in the early 1990s receiving training through him and his team. The teaching was outstanding, but the highlight of the program were the activations, activations, and more activations. The sessions included strong coaching, exhortation, and encouragement to prophesy. We all responded! Those who had never prophesied in their life were now flowing in the prophetic. Bishop Hamon's books and teachings continue to train, equip, and mentor the gifts and the character of those who prophesy. In addition to all this, you can easily discern his father's heart because he carries the heart of the Father.

Leaders

Benjamin Deitrick

As we define spiritual fathers and mothers, sons and daughters, and mentors, it's also important to define those who hold a leadership office or other roles in our lives. These different roles can be confusing to some people. They believe that if a leader is in their lives, whether in a business or church role, then they must be either a mentor or spiritual parent. Some believe they must make themselves feel a certain closeness or admiration for these people and often feel guilty when these feelings don't come.

But the nature of the roles is different. A spiritual father or mother will bring with them closeness and intimacy. A mentor will bring excitement and growth within the context of what is being learned and experienced. On the other hand, a leader is someone who, among other things, provides oversight, structure, and knowledge; there is often no emotion, closeness, or excitement in it. But that doesn't mean they don't serve a purpose. Every leader who comes into our lives serves a purpose, and we are to yield to and celebrate that in whatever way we can. Sometimes you will have an overlap in which a leader is also a spiritual father or mother, or mentor, but it's not always the case.

A leader is defined as One who leads or commands a group, organization, or country. Leaders are those who have acquired skills to lead over the course of a professional journey.

Leaders are very diverse in their roles and responsibilities. They can be our boss, a head usher at church, team leader, or other. We have leaders over us in the nations and regions we live in such as governors, senators, and prime ministers. Leaders can be found in the church, government, business, education, and in every realm of activity in society.

Spiritual leaders oversee people or a specific assignment or area of ministry. We are taught in scripture to obey leaders and submit to their authority. They are always to be treated with respect and honor. Again, this respect and honor do not have to include closeness or intimacy in any way.

Romans 13:1–5 (NIV)

Let everyone be subject to the governing authorities, for there is no authority except that which God has established. The authorities that exist have been established by God. Consequently, whoever rebels against the authority is rebelling against what God has instituted, and those who do so will bring judgment on themselves. For rulers hold no terror for those who do right, but for those who do wrong. Do you want to be free from fear of the one in authority? Then do what is right and you will be commended. For the one in authority is God's servant for your good. But if you do wrong, be afraid, for rulers do not bear the sword for no reason. They are God's servants, agents of wrath to bring punishment on the wrongdoer. Therefore, it is necessary to submit to the authorities, not only because of possible punishment but also as a matter of conscience.

I really appreciate the language the Bible uses here, which tells us that our obedience to leaders (in whatever role) is a matter of conscience. Simply put, obeying leaders and submitting in a godly way to their authority is a basic part of a believer's life. It's the right thing to do. Some of us would have so much more peace in our jobs or in our life in general if we could understand this. You do not need to like your leaders; you do not need to feel close to them, but you do need to obey them! Many times we choose, or the Lord chooses for us, spiritual fathers, mothers, and mentors. Leaders are different; we don't usually choose them, they are assigned to us.

The Bible further speaks of leaders through Peter:

1 Peter 2:13-17 (NIV)

Submit yourselves for the Lord's sake to every human authority: whether to the emperor, as the supreme authority, or to governors, who are sent by him to punish those who do wrong and to commend those who do right. For it is God's will that by doing good you should silence the ignorant talk of foolish people. Live as free people, but do not use your freedom as a cover-up for evil; live as God's

---

Simply put, obeying leaders and submitting in a godly way to their authority is a basic part of the life of a believer. It's the right thing to do.

---

slaves. Show proper respect to everyone, love the family of believers, fear God, honor the emperor.

The main focus here is that "human authority" is a part of everyone's life. We are to respect these leaders regardless of what sector of society they operate in—church, business, government, etc.—as well as our spiritual fathers and mothers, the spiritual assignments and authorities sent to us by God.

Hebrews 13:17 says,

Obey your leaders and submit to them, for they are keeping watch over your souls, as those who will have to give an account. Let them do this with joy and not with groaning, for that would be of no advantage to you. (ESV)

The word used for "leader" here, basically boils down to a "chief"—one who commands or oversees. It is very different from the word Paul uses for "father" in 1 Corinthians 4:15, which is *patér* (phonetic: pat-ayr'), meaning one who imparts life and is committed to it.

In conclusion, a father/mother imparts life and is committed to sustaining and nurturing it. A mentor imparts information and knowledge and helps to empower you to walk in it. A leader is one who oversees an area of vision, assignment, or responsibility. They issue directives and expect them to be obeyed. A leader can also be a spiritual mother, father, or mentor, but not always. There are unique differences between all three, and it hinges on primary purpose and assignment.

CONVERSATION POINT

Discuss the importance of mentors and leaders to aid in the turning of the hearts of the generations to one another.

ACTIVATION

Make a list of the many mentors and leaders the Holy Spirit has used in your spiritual development and the areas in which they have impacted you. Take some time before the Lord to thank Him for using these vessels as mentors in your spiritual development and growth.

Chapter Six

WHAT IS A SPIRITUAL CHILD?

Benjamin Deitrick

I have been both a spiritual child and parent and have experienced the maturing processes that both bring.

In my walk with God, I am blessed and privileged to have received so much through spiritual mothers and fathers. I will never forget the moment I was saved and filled with the Holy Spirit. A huge battle was raging inside my soul that evening. I had received the Lord as a child and had learned a lot about the Bible and the concepts of God, but my heart had drifted and become hard. I was hanging out with a terrible crowd and had begun a downward spiral toward a life of rebellion. My life was hanging in the balance, and I could easily have ruined it permanently by decisions I was planning to make that night until God intervened.

A spiritual father and mother pulled me out of darkness, brought me back into a living relationship with Jesus, and presented Him to me in a way where He became real to my heart and more than simply a concept. My life was never the same as I was "re-born" in Jesus that night and filled with the power of the Holy Spirit. Spiritual parents incubated, birthed, and helped me establish my life in God.

In previous chapters, Patricia has written extensively about spiritual parents, but what is a spiritual child? Does age define it? Are you a spiritual child simply because you are young? Do you stay a spiritual child all your life, or are there seasons of learning and development in this stage?

What Does It Mean to Be a Spiritual Child?

Nicodemus asked Jesus questions about entering the Kingdom of God in John 3:1-9. Jesus responded by saying you must be spiritually born into this Kingdom. When we receive Christ as our Savior, God, Himself, becomes our Father, and we are His child. A spiritual child is birthed by the Spirit of God and belongs to God.

Every new baby needs love, celebration, care, and nurture, and your Father in heaven lavishes each of His children with all these attributes. He has engraved your name on the palms of His hands (Isaiah 49:16). Being a spiritual child means you belong to Him. It is not what you do but who you are and Whose you are.

Just as a natural child learns, grows, and develops according to their age, a spiritual child learns, grows, and progresses through many stages in their journey. God begins to nurture you with the basics and then progresses.

> **Just as a natural child learns, grows, and develops according to their age, a spiritual child learns, grows, and progresses through many stages in their journey.**

Just as an infant begins with only milk in their diet, so all of us who are in Christ have started our journey with the "milk of His Word." We didn't come out of the spiritual "womb" full-grown any more than a baby comes out of their mother's womb full-grown. The Lord can mature you rapidly in ways that far supersede the example of a natural child.

In my opinion, this depends primarily on your hunger level and how much you apply what you are learning/receiving. A natural infant who is hungry and feeds often will grow quickly. You can mature quickly in Christ or remain a child your whole life. The power lies with you.

Several times in scripture, the Apostle Paul defines himself not only as a father in the Lord, but he also identifies several people as "spiritual sons" whom he has "begotten" in the Lord. There are several Greek words used for "child" or "son" in the scriptures, and there are unique keys for us to derive from their meanings. Let's look at some of these as they relate to spiritual children.

It says in 1 Timothy 1:2:

To Timothy my true son in the faith: Grace, mercy and peace from God the Father and Christ Jesus our Lord. (NIV)

The word for son here is the word *teknon* (phonetic: tek'non). It means a child (of either sex), a descendant, one who is living in full dependence of a father/mother in glad submission.

Teknon, however, is not to be used exclusively for a beginning stage or a stage of full dependence and immaturity but can also be understood as a phrase used to convey endearment. I believe Paul addressed Timothy with this word as a term of endearment. Paul lovingly walked with Timothy as he was being molded and formed in the ways of Christ. As we know, Timothy was later entrusted with much authority and responsibility, especially in Ephesus, which was at one time the second biggest city of the entire Roman empire. In 1 Timothy 4:12, Paul had to exhort Timothy to not let anyone look down on him due to his youth or age because of the scope of what Timothy had been entrusted with.

Even though we cannot assign the word *teknon* to a specific stage of maturity, we can determine that there are different levels of maturity within our journey as spiritual children.

Another meaning of *teknon* is "a disciple." When we are first saved, we require constant encouragement, teaching, training, and discipling. The *teknon* is one who is "walking in the dust of their Rabbi."[4] In other words, wherever the teacher/spiritual parent goes and whatever they do, the *teknon* is to imitate. Paul demonstrates this principle powerfully in 1 Corinthians 4:16, "So I urge you, be imitators of me [just as a child imitates his father].

---

4 "May You Be Covered with the Dust of your Rabbi" by Tim Bartee. https://www.sidneydailynews.com/news/religion/48792/may-you-be-covered-with-the-dust-of-your-rabbi

A spiritual child should not despise or skip this stage in the maturing process. At some point in our walk with God, we will have matured and moved on past that stage of needing constant care and nurture. However, even as we mature, there may be specific areas where we still need to position ourselves again as a *teknon*—to make our minds and hearts a blank slate again, positioned in humility to learn what we need in that area of our development.

In the *teknon* phase, a spiritual child is learning foundational elements—the basics of life and godliness. Some of these are described in Hebrews chapter 6 which specifically mentions some of the foundational elements of our faith in Christ.

Hebrews 6:1-2 (KJV)

> Therefore leaving the principles of the doctrine of Christ, let us go on unto perfection; not laying again the foundation of repentance from dead works, and of faith toward God, Of the doctrine of baptisms, and of laying on of hands, and of resurrection of the dead, and of eternal judgment.

Paul invites us to move on "unto perfection." This is an ideal segue into the next word we will look at in the developmental stages of being a spiritual child—the word *telios* (phonetic: tel'-i-os).

This word means "having reached its end, complete, perfect, full grown, of full age."

Paul is also not saying we leave or abandon the elementary doctrines and practices of faith, but rather that we move onward and upward into full maturity and effective service in Christ. He means that we cannot remain there.

Imagine a house being built where only the foundation is laid. You might be able to enjoy some limited use on the foundation, but the full purpose of the house would not be realized or utilized.

Imagine a building with no foundation. That would be an unstable, weak structure that could be easily destroyed. Likewise, spiritual foundations are essential, but we also must build on those foundations. Milk offers great nourishment for infants, but as you develop, you need heftier meals.

I see it like this: the foundational elements focus on what Christ has done for us—His perfect sacrifice and the call for us to believe and receive what He's done. The more mature features are when we are called to implement, live, and teach those things, laying our lives down in like manner to Christ.

We begin with what is *for us* and then move on to what is ***through us*** which requires a greater level of sacrifice. It's not about one being better than the other, but rather a different application and assignment, depending on the stage of our journey. That is why we are not to despise the *teknon* stage but to fully embrace it. However, we must move on to greater sacrifice and surrender of our lives, following Christ's example.

This word *telios* in the following verses will give you greater context and understanding of how and where it is used.

Jesus says in Matthew 5:48 to *be "perfect" as your Father in heaven is perfect.* I remember reading this as a child and thinking, "I can never live up to that!" But there's good news! You are not being called to be perfect in the sense that the western world understands it. It is a call to be mature and Christlike. To grow from milk to meat. To walk in Christ's example.

Romans 12:2 is another example:

> Do not conform to the pattern of this world, but be transformed by the renewing of your mind. Then you will be able to test and approve what God's will is—his good, pleasing and perfect will. (NIV)

The same word is used here for the "perfect" will of God. We can rightly understand and perceive the perfect (mature, full-grown) will of God when we are mature and full-grown in our faith.

During the *teknon* stage, the foundation of Christ is being built in us, and then the walls can go up after that foundation is in place and secure. His work of maturity beautifies the home of our hearts and lives. We can then move and operate in our *function*, ultimately discerning God's will for our lives and imparting wisdom to others as well.

Another noteworthy word is found in Romans 8:19. It reads:

> For the creation waits in eager expectation for the children of God to be revealed. (NIV)

The word for children here is *huios* (phonetic: hwee-os'). It means son, child, descendant, or anyone sharing the same **nature** as their Father; their lives reflect His character. Once again, this concept applies to women as much as men even though it is written in a male context. Men are as much the "Bride of Christ"(Ephesians 5) as women are "sons of God" through faith in Christ Jesus. Galatians 3:26-28 makes this very clear:

> For you are all sons of God through faith in Christ Jesus. For as many of you as were baptized into Christ have put on Christ. There is neither Jew nor Greek, there is neither slave nor free, there is neither male nor female; for you are all one in Christ Jesus.

This same word, *huios,* is the word that is used in John 3:16, "For God so loved the world that he sent his only begotten ***son...***" Jesus was sent as the image of God, one sharing His exact nature, a mature son.

Isn't that powerful! The earth itself is longing for mature children of God to be manifested and revealed. Where do they come from and who do they belong to? GOD! Not to any person, not even to a spiritual father or mother, no matter how anointed or influential these persons may be. However, spiritual fathers and mothers are to reflect THE Father in heaven and bring their spiritual children into maturity in the Lord. The spiritual child has to be willing to be molded. Being a spiritual child has nothing to do with age, gender, race, etc., but rather with maturity, hunger, humility, and a heart willing to learn and be molded by the Spirit.

Isn't that powerful! The earth itself is longing for mature children of God to be manifested and revealed.

Do You Remain a Spiritual Child All Your Life?

I personally believe that the Lord gives spiritual fathers and mothers to spiritual children as representatives of His own love, grace, and mercy. There are seasons for these relationships. God sets the parameters and the length of time for these seasons. I have had the blessing of being discipled by five spiritual fathers/mothers in my life. These people are more than simply mentors from whom I have learned; rather, I've received and am still receiving an impartation of life from them.

The Bible says that the Word of God is like seed. The word used for seed is *sperma:* seed which is sown that produces life. A spiritual parent has the power to impart life from the Word of God just as a natural parent possesses this power to produce life. The life is in the seed, just as it is described even in the fruit of the Garden of Eden in Genesis 1:12. The seeds produce according to their kind.

There is power in this, but it is also a warning for spiritual parents and children; whatever you sow into your spiritual children you will reproduce in them according to **what is in you**. It's the law of leadership; we don't reproduce what we ***desire***, we reproduce according to ***what we are***. There is a sobriety in this that all of us should heed.

So, God appoints and sets this season of sowing and growing together as spiritual parents/children, and no one can tell how long it is going to be. There are some who have been blessed by God with a primary spiritual parent with whom they are in close relationship their entire lives. God appoints this, and it is wonderful. However, I don't believe everyone has only one spiritual father or mother over the course of their life. Rather, you have one primary voice and parent in your life in a particular God-appointed season.

In the hearts of spiritual parents and their spiritual child, there will (should) always be love, honor, and respect for each other in those roles, but roles shift and change as people mature. Many spiritual parents make the mistake of trying to keep their spiritual children in the same roles for too long. In some cases, I have observed that the season has shifted, maturity has come, and the assignment has been fulfilled, but for whatever reason, the spiritual parent seeks to hold on. On the other hand, the spiritual child sometimes holds on past the season. This does not produce good fruit; in fact, many times it becomes co-dependent.

Imagine a child that never leaves home; instead, their parents continue to provide everything for them, cook their meals, clean the house, and wash their clothes even into their 30s, 40s, and 50s. They are stunted in their growth and maturity and never learn to govern their own home because they remain dependent on their parents far beyond the appropriate time. The same applies to spiritual parenting. Every spiritual parent must be willing to let go and not "own" their spiritual children. Likewise, the spiritual child must be willing to take responsibility and move into maturity, not "own" their spiritual parent for the sake of influence, selfish ambition, or gain.

In this phase of growth, even though spiritual parents will always be honored as such, the relationship of the mature son or daughter with his/her spiritual parent moves into friendship and more of a peer relationship as co-heirs in Christ when the Lord shifts the season.

This concept is demonstrated in the life of Christ at the time of His baptism in Matthew 3:16, "As soon as Jesus was baptized, he went up out of the water. At that moment heaven was opened, and he saw the Spirit of God descending like a dove and alighting on him. And a voice from heaven said, "This is my Son, whom I love; with him I am well pleased." (NIV)

At this time in history, in Jewish culture, when a son had come of age, the father would take that son to the gates of the city where all legal transactions took place. He would bring his son before the other men/leaders of the city and make the same declaration that Father God made of Jesus in Matthew 3, "This is my beloved son. I am well pleased with him. Listen to him!"

From that time forward, the son had the same standing and authority as the father. The son never lost his identity as the son, the father never lost his identity as the father, but there was an acknowledgment of maturity, and with it came authority. The son could buy and sell, engage in legal transactions, and more.

Notice that following this endorsement from the Father, Christ's ministry began. The declaration was made from heaven, and the Spirit of God came and empowered Christ to operate fully in the earth as the Father did. The rest is history, but the principle is still true for us today. We are ALL sons of God through faith in Christ Jesus. The Father is the Father of us all. We need to be willing to move with God in and out of the seasons of parenting and being a child with joy! It is a pleasure and an honor to be His spiritual child!

CONVERSATION POINT

Discuss the topic of having more than one spiritual parent in the course of your life. What are your thoughts on this and why?

ACTIVATION

1. What areas of your life do you identify as being in the *Teknon* (dependent child) stage?
2. What areas of your life do you see yourself in the *Telios* (mature believer) stage?
3. What areas of your life do you see yourself in the *Huios* (Christlike) stage?

Chapter Seven

FIVE IMPORTANT ATTRIBUTES OF A SPIRITUAL CHILD

Benjamin Deitrick

In this chapter, I will outline five key attributes in spiritual children that create healthy and fruitful relationships with spiritual parents.

This is not an exhaustive list, but rather my own perspective on the five that I perceive to be most vital. As you read through these, the Lord may highlight some additional attributes that you want to take note of and implement in your life as a spiritual son or daughter.

1. Honor

The concepts of honor in both the Old and New Testaments are so linked with the glory of the Lord that it is basically impossible to separate them. In Hebrew, the main word that is translated as glory is *kabod*. The word for honor is *kabed*. They are so similar that sometimes they have been interchanged with one another. In Greek it's the same thing. The word glory is *doxa* and the word for honor is *doxazo*. The point I am trying to make is that you cannot have glory without honor.

How many times have you been in a church service and either heard a message or seen an altar call rallying the people of God to cry out for more glory in their lives and in the church? I have seen it repeatedly. Yet, it seems that in many ways we see honor diminishing, not only in our society but also in church culture. Is it possible to have a sweeping move of revival and glory, the wind, fire, and oil of the Holy Spirit when we do not have a culture of honor? I don't believe so.

While I believe there have been abuses of power in church leadership, I also see the other side of the coin—that the fathers and mothers of our generation are not always appropriately honored. Because of this, when I look at the future generations, I am concerned about the level of glory and anointing that will be able to be poured out upon them and in their midst because there is no structure of honor to host the glory. Divine structures and order produce God's glory! Without the structure of honor, there is no wineskin to host the glory of God.

Honor doesn't look like flattery or self-abasement and false humility. Kingdom honor looks very different. It is rooted in honor of God first and then in turn, honor of those people who God places "over us" in the Lord. Ephesians 6:1-3 says:

> Children, obey your parents in the Lord, for this is right. "Honor your father and mother"—which is the first

commandment with a promise—"so that it may go well with you and that you may enjoy long life on the earth." (NIV)

This verse speaks of honoring natural parents, but I believe it applies to spiritual parents as well. Romans 12:10 says, "Be devoted to one another in love. Honor one another above yourselves." (NIV)

If you are to walk as a beloved spiritual child, you will honor your spiritual parents from your heart. The outward expression of that will be directed by the leading of your heart and the Holy Spirit. It isn't something that can be formalized or set in stone. Some show honor by serving in practical ways—some bless financially, some honor with words, and the list goes on. There are multitudes of ways to honor, but true honor flows from the heart and is not linked to performance or the desire to earn recognition or rights. The Kingdom of God isn't quid pro quo which means "something for something." Freely we have received, freely we give!

God loves honor, and when honor is activated, it produces glory and favor. Dishonor, on the other hand, produces disqualification. I have sadly seen spiritual children dishonor spiritual parents and leaders. As a result, they have been hindered in their spiritual growth and well-being in life. Genesis 9:18-29 reveals Noah's son Ham dishonoring him by uncovering his nakedness.

God loves honor, and when honor is activated, it produces glory and favor. Dishonor, on the other hand, produces disqualification.

A curse came on Ham's life following. This is not to suggest that criminal, inhumane behaviors or acts of injustice should be ignored, but when they are brought to the light, it must be in the fear of the Lord and not carelessly executed.

2. Hunger

I will never forget one day after church in the Pennsylvanian community where I was raised. I was racing my friend Bruce behind the church. We were going time after time, race after race, and every single time he was beating me! At one point I noticed my father coming over to watch. He was trying to catch my eye and eventually called me over to him. He asked, "How hungry are you to win this race?" And I said, "I don't know, Dad…I might as well give up, he beats me every time." He looked at me intently and said, "You will never win with that attitude! Get hungry to win. Get focused! I believe you can beat him if you set your mind to it and *don't give up*." That encouragement was all I needed. I went back into that race, set my eyes on the finish line, and gave it all I had. My hunger drove me, and I won!

My father's encouragement was what gave me victory that day! My "opponent" who was also my friend had beaten me time after time, but I never gave up. When I won the first time, I kept on winning after that. I had tasted the sweet blessing of victory, and it made me hungry for more. A spiritual parent encourages and imparts hope and wisdom, but the spiritual child must be hungry to receive and apply that encouragement for it to be effective.

I believe so much of our life in God hinges on hunger. Barbara Yoder was one of the spiritual parents I was blessed to walk with for many years. When speaking of deliverance ministry, she always said, "Deliverance is for the desperate." In other words, if you approach deliverance ministry with a halfhearted attitude, you will receive very little freedom. It's like asking someone bound in chains and imprisoned if they want to be free and that prisoner saying, "Hmmm … well … I don't know …" Would that person ever seize an opportunity to be free? No! They would probably not see an opportunity for freedom even if it flashed before their eyes, because they have no hunger to be free!

Hunger is paramount. Have you ever been extremely hungry but unable to eat, either because you didn't have the money or because you didn't have access to food? Maybe you have fasted extensively. I remember the first time I fasted … Oh, boy! What a beneficial spiritual discipline, but not easy, at least for me. I was 16 years old and partook in a "30-Hour Famine" with other youth group kids. I had rededicated my life to Jesus, and I was so on fire! But this was hard! I didn't eat anything in those 30 hours, but then I came home like a little ravenous wolf. My mother asked me if I was okay, and I said, "Mom, I felt like I was going to die!"

It's funny now, looking back on it as someone who has done several longer fasts over the years, to think I was "going to die" after only 30 hours. But that is the power of hunger!

As a father of three wonderful daughters, I love to feed them and see them fully satisfied when they share that they are hungry. On the other hand, when they are not hungry, it isn't easy to make them eat. Spiritual children who are hungry will be fed. It is a delight to feed those who are spiritually hungry.

Jesus said in Luke 6:21 that hunger is a blessing. If you are filled, you hunger for nothing. As spiritual children, hunger for the Lord, righteousness, truth, and all the Spirit longs to give. Hunger for more! When you are hungry, there is a promise of a feast!

3. Servanthood

Jesus was a perfect Son to His Father in heaven and is our most excellent and most reliable example of sonship (including daughtership.) As a Son, He modeled servanthood perfectly. He came as God in the flesh, not to be served but to serve (Mark 10:45).

Isaiah prophesied of Him in chapter 53, a portion often titled "The Suffering Servant." He gave Himself as a ransom for many and poured His life out with great sacrifice for the benefit of all of us. What a Servant!

As a spiritual Son, we find Him in the Garden of Gethsemane in deep, anguished intercession, yielding His will to serve the Father's desires, declaring, "Not My will but Yours" (Luke 22:42).

Servanthood is one of the most defining characteristics of spiritual maturity and service. Many see this concept of servanthood as being diminished or abased, when in fact, it is the path to true authority. Philippians 2 makes this so clear for us.

Philippians 2:8-9

And being found in appearance as a man, he humbled himself by becoming obedient to death—even death on a cross!

> **Jesus taught that the greatest in the Kingdom is the servant, and He was the servant of all.**

Therefore God exalted him to the highest place and gave him the name that is above every name.

Jesus taught that the greatest in the Kingdom is the servant, and He was the servant of all!

Mark 10:42-45 (NASB1995)

Calling them to Himself, Jesus said to them, 'You know that those who are recognized as rulers of the Gentiles domineer over them; and their people in high position exercise authority over them. But it is not this way among you; rather, whoever wants to become prominent among you shall be your servant; and whoever wants to be first among you shall be slave of all. For even the Son of Man did not come to be served, but to serve, and to give His life as a ransom for many.

The Holy Spirit is poured out in the last days on God's servants. Acts 2:18, "And even on My male and female servants I will pour out My Spirit in those days."

We see examples in scripture such as Elisha serving Elijah. Elisha was a spiritual son of Elijah and referred to him as "father." From the moment Elijah called him, he served him well (1 Kings 19:19-21). Many scholars believe that they walked together for six years before Elijah departed. To that very moment, Elisha was a faithful servant and following, took up Elijah's mantle and performed twice the miracles Elijah did.

I had the privilege of serving two amazing leaders over the course of around 20 years. Robert Stearns and Barbara Yoder have both been spiritual parents as well as amazing mentors in my life. In early 2022, my season of pastoring at Shekinah, led and founded by Barbara Yoder, came to an end, and the Lord birthed and entrusted a new ministry to my wife and me. In this journey of serving others in their ministries and then being entrusted with my own ministry to lead, there has been nothing more important to me than the mindset of servanthood.

I remember being very young, around 18 years old, when Robert Stearns first called me to his office and told me that he had a "ministry assignment" for me to oversee. I was very excited (and actually full of delusions of grandeur!). I expected him to tell me that after my voluminous amount of time and faithful service to Eagles Wings (two months) that he was entrusting me to go on the road as his representative and preach and teach in the USA and the nations of the earth. This was my moment—and it was—but not the moment I anticipated.

He told me that I was to serve as the head of… (drum roll please)… the snow crew. I was to form a team of willing people to shovel all five driveways of the ministry's property and to make sure that all the snow was clear in the mornings before the morning devotions (8 am) and throughout the day. This was in Buffalo, NY, a place where it snows for seven months out of the year sometimes. When he said this to me, I immediately sobered up! I spent the next several months faithfully serving in this way, often alone, for several hours throughout the day. One day as I was pushing some especially heavy snow off one of the driveways, I threw my shovel down in frustration and asked the Lord the proverbial, "What are you doing to me?" He answered very clearly in that moment, "I am building your character before I release your ministry. I'm teaching you what ministry is all about, son."

I will never forget that moment as long as I live. He made it so clear to me. I picked my shovel back up, put my head down, and served. I served in this and many other practical ways through those years and have come to enjoy and love serving in "menial" ways as much as I enjoy preaching to hundreds of people. I learned then that servanthood was not a "season," a "one-time thing," something we graduate from, or even a test … It is a lifestyle that Christ calls us to; one that reflects His own. It is to be a key motivation behind all we do. There is glory in serving, and a spiritual child must have this as a part of their core foundation. We are called to serve with joy!

4. Honesty

Honesty is vital. I have been hurt and have also hurt spiritual mothers and fathers because I wasn't honest. I didn't want to be rejected, overlooked, demeaned, or disciplined, so I held back much of what I thought and felt. I would politely agree with what was being communicated rather than giving my honest input. I often tried to toe the line and be the "perfect son," but ultimately I bottled up internal wrestles when boundaries in my heart or life were crossed. Unfortunately, it would come out in either anger or frustration later. This wasn't helpful to either my spiritual parents or me.

This "perfection" mindset comes primarily out of two things: fear of rejection and idolizing spiritual parents.

The Psalmist says in Psalm 51:6, "Surely You desire truth in the inmost being; You teach me wisdom in the inmost place." We are all on a journey toward this—to know the truth deep inside.

Jesus declared that He is the embodiment of truth. In John 14:6, Jesus says, "I am the way and the truth and the life. No one comes to the Father except through me." This word "truth" (Greek: *alétheia,* phonetic: al-ay'-thi-a) has an amazing, multi-faceted meaning. One of the main ways to understand it is "reality." So Jesus literally declared, "I am your reality!" As believers, we are to live from this place of Christ's reality. In His reality, there is nothing hidden or lying in darkness. We can be honoring and yet totally honest with our thoughts, convictions, and opinions, operating from the heart of Christ.

If we are to walk in a healthy manner in the spiritual parent/child relationship, there must be openness and honest communication. Some of the greatest freedom I have ever experienced came when I was open with a spiritual parent and totally honest about the parts of me that I thought were the "worst." When I was open and honest, the fear of rejection and the need for performance and perfection fell off of me. Instead of being met

---

If we are to walk in a healthy manner in the spiritual parent/child relationship, there must be openness and honest communication.

---

with rejection and shame after exposing the struggles of my soul, I was met with love and acceptance!

The other aspect is idolizing leaders. This isn't pleasant but it needs to be addressed. There has been confusion and, in some cases, abuse in the body of Christ because spiritual parents or leaders were given a place of authority and control that crossed godly ethics, values, and biblical understanding. There is a school of thought or a mindset in some denominations and movements that you are never to submit your honest questions, concerns, or convictions to your spiritual parent because they always know what is right and you are always wrong. In some extreme situations, you are taught to listen and obey no matter what is being said to you or how it violates your conscience. This can shut down the soul, abuse the mind, and is an unhealthy model. It allows for easy manipulation, intimidation, domination, and control. This type of behavior opens lives to deception, bondage, and oppression, and it is literally how cults form. Some of you, thankfully, might not relate to this or understand it, but to others it rings home in a heartfelt, experiential way.

We need to create safe environments in our generation. We don't want to repeatedly end up with more and more broken hearts and people. If you are reading this and you find yourself in a spiritual parenting relationship where you are afraid to be honest, you need to ask yourself some hard questions. It could be an issue of fear in your own life in which you need healing, or you could be in an unhealthy situation where the will of another is dominating your own.

The Lord never dominates the will of His people. He calls us to volitional love, honor, and service. Likewise, it is never the will of the Lord for spiritual parents to take away choice and free will in the lives of those they parent or abuse their place of authority in any way. Spiritual parents or leaders are never to be idolized or put above the Word and will of the Lord.

On the other side of this scenario of idolatry, there are younger generation individuals who will not listen or process in truth and love with a spiritual parent. Sometimes they are rudely confrontational. They disrespect their leaders through accusation and condemnation and have discerned the hearts of their leaders incorrectly because they failed to hear the hearts of their leaders and listen well. Sometimes the root of this type of behavior is self-idolatry.

We all need to be open, vulnerable, and honest with each other—with a heart of love, humility, and respect. This is how we turn our hearts to each other.

5. Humility

Philippians 2:3-4 says,

Do nothing out of selfish ambition or vain conceit, but in humility consider others better than yourselves. Each of you should look not only to your own interests, but also to the interests of others. (NIV)

At the time of this writing, I have been in full-time ministry for over 20 years. I have seen so much beauty expressed through the people of God that has touched and changed my heart forever. I love being a minister, and I love being a Christian! Unfortunately, I have also observed many things that I believe grieve the heart of God. One of those things is self-promotion.

Self-promotion is defined as "the action of promoting or publicizing oneself or one's activities, especially in a forceful way." This isn't something new or unique to our time, but I do feel it's been exacerbated by the "selfie" social media culture we live in. We're encouraged now to "put yourself out there, be your best self, and live your best life." Self-love is promoted as healthy and necessary. While there is a point to loving and caring for yourself, there is an overemphasis that is producing a lot of entitlement. This mindset has invaded the world and the church. There is an entire culture that has now emerged in the Body of Christ that is built on the back of networking, pandering for favor and influence with those we deem influential, and the overall promotion and elevation of *self*.

I have seen this invade the spiritual parent/child culture, and a push has emerged for people to identify spiritual parents, not for the purpose of discipleship in Christ, but to associate with them for advancement and promotion in ministry. The feeling is one of rabid action and attention, jostling for position, beating out the other person to "get there first" to the person of influence who can help you "make it in ministry" and "expose you to the world." This is not the Kingdom model or pattern. This is a man-made, fleshly, carnal system that is built on entitlement, selfish ambition, and pride. It is not the way of a disciple in Jesus Christ.

> **The call comes to all of us to walk in the footsteps of our Master and to die to our own reputation, desires, lusts, and need for significance.**

I have used the example of ministry but the same is happening in the business world, in politics, and in every other sector of society.

Here is the Lord's call to us as spiritual children:

Philippians 2:5-8

Let this mind be in you which was also in Christ Jesus, who, being in the form of God, did not consider it robbery to be equal with God, but made Himself of no reputation, taking the form of a bondservant, and coming in the likeness of men. And being found in appearance as a man, He humbled Himself and became obedient to the point of death, even the death of the cross.

The call to humility does not come to those who are concerned about their reputation and influence in this life. The call comes to all of us to walk in the footsteps of our Master and to DIE to our own reputation, desires, lusts, and need for significance. We are to live lives that are surrendered to Him and Him alone.

If we are to walk as godly spiritual children, we must never through vain conceit use spiritual parents for selfish ends. We must walk in the humility of Christ. If we humble ourselves, He will exalt us in due time (1 Peter 5:6).

This doesn't mean we shrink back from receiving promotion or enjoying influence when the Lord offers that. But who gets the glory? And for what eternal Kingdom purpose is that influence given? I have discovered that any increase in influence or promotion received is actually an invitation to deeper sacrifice and service. At the end of the day, we all want to hear only one thing: "Well done good and faithful **servant**."

We are all looking forward to that moment of affirmation from our true Father, and nothing can ever take it away! Let us live for that and that alone, and let our relationships be built on genuine love, honor, and humility.

CONVERSATION POINT

Discuss the importance of these attributes in the younger generation as they relate to the older generation and share additional attributes that you deem important.

ACTIVATION

Note the attributes in which you are already functioning and also those in which you need to grow. Pray for the Lord to establish these attributes in your life.

Chapter Eight

GENERATIONS GROWING IN RELATIONSHIP

Patricia King

For the hearts of the fathers to turn to the next generation, and the next generation to the fathers, both must be determined to grow together in Christ, appreciating and honoring each other. Often you hear people talking about a "generation gap" or one generation complaining about the flaws of the other.

I don't believe there should be any gap in the generations. The Lord is the God of Abraham, Isaac, and Jacob and not the God of Abraham, gap, Isaac, gap, and Jacob, gap. Although each generation is unique and carries different assignments, we must see each other in Christ, partnering and running together seamlessly for the advancement of His Kingdom and glory. He is coming for one glorious church, filled with believers who love and honor each other. God requires the hearts of the fathers to turn to the children and the children to the fathers, and that is exactly what we intend to give Him.

As we grow in our relationship with each other, there are some keys and dynamics the Spirit of God has taught me along the way that might be helpful to you.

Stop, Look, Listen

If we are going to build healthy relationships generationally, there are things that we need to **STOP**, such as some of the labels that are being proclaimed over the generations. For example, some of the common judgments over the millennials are that they are self-entitled and obsessed, lack persistence and endurance, are financially irresponsible, feel like the world owes them, prefer making their own schedule without consideration of others, and naively believe they know how to properly run the world and its affairs. You don't have to search far to discover these generalized judgments; they are easily found on the internet—just Google it.

I can testify that I work with many millennials and have had a totally different experience with them. They are hard-working, attentive, honoring, and responsible. Secondly, proclaiming negative and accusative judgments doesn't make one a better person but, instead, lays a word curse over their life. This must **STOP** if we are going to turn our hearts to each other.

I have also heard the younger generation openly judging the older generation with statements such as they are performance-obsessed, workaholics, driven, careless about the environment and how it affects future generations, politically dogmatic, and they hold to a belief that life and success are measured by money and material possessions. Some baby boomers reading this might be reeling in defense right now and ready to

> **Proclaiming negative and accusative judgments doesn't make one a better person but simply lays a word curse over their life. This must STOP if we are going to turn our hearts to each other.**

retaliate—which is not a righteous response—but this type of judgment is not beneficial for the turning of the hearts to one another. It is not a full perspective, it is not honoring. It won't bear righteous fruit, and it must **STOP**.

Let's stop judging, devaluing, and faulting each other, and instead, **LOOK** for the nature of Christ in each one. Let's put our love lenses on and view each other through the Lord's eyes. If you **LOOK**, you will see. **LOOK** beyond the faults, failings, and shortcomings, and see the full potential in each other. If you perceive a person in a negative light, they will always be that to you. God always **LOOKS** beyond our flaws and sees destiny, purpose, and potential. Let's be like Him.

LISTEN to what each other is carrying. If we are not open to what another has to say, we will never expand our understanding. Even if you don't agree with someone, **LISTEN** to what they communicate. I have discovered that when I listen well, I learn much, and areas of dogmatic perceptions sometimes shift in the light of what is shared. You will never hear if you don't **LISTEN**. As I have sat through many sessions with people who struggled with each other, the main key to breakthrough was that each one **LISTENED** well to the other.

Sincerely **LISTEN** from a place of empathy to all that another is communicating—put yourself in their shoes and attempt to perceive the situation from their understanding. You might not agree with everything, but these are the beliefs that are real to them at the time. To build a relationship, overcome conflicts, and grow together, we must **LISTEN** and value their hearts.

Establishing Values

God taught me years ago to build our ministry on a foundation of Kingdom values and not on vision or doctrine. Your vision and assignments can change over time, and even though solid biblical beliefs in your life and ministry are essential, your interpretation and application of biblical truth can expand or even be adjusted over time. (For example, some believers were taught in their church that the gifts of the Spirit are not for today and later realized they are.) Kingdom values, however, remain constant. Our ministry has been blessed with this foundation. We might violate a value, but because we are committed to the value, we can address it and come back to the plumbline. It aids us with self-accountability and helps us hold each other accountable in love.

When building relationships between the generations, it is beneficial to establish values of unconditional love, forgiveness, adherence to uncompromised truth, humility, honesty, teachability, honor, and servanthood to name a few. If values are defined, understood, and agreed upon, even when you have differences, disagreements, or shortcomings, there is a Kingdom framework to adhere to. You can address the violation and call each other back.

Imagine the generations committing to Kingdom values as they relate to one another. Perhaps you would like to establish specific values in your own life right now. Values that you adhere to as you commit to turning your heart to the other generation. One by one, we could bring about a change. Take time now to make a list of values you choose to be accountable to.

The Power of Processing

Conflicts and disagreements happen in life, but everything can usually be resolved if all parties involved are willing to process until peace comes. You might not come into full agreement, but you will establish peace between you as you adhere to non-negotiable love.

Processing takes the ability to communicate honestly without malice and to sincerely listen to each other. Sometimes a mediator is required, and if so, do whatever it takes to bring resolution to the conflict.

Often with generational connections, there are differences in building vision or Kingdom assignments. The older generation has been led by the Lord in a particular way over the years, and they see things through that perspective while the younger generation is being directed differently.

In 2010, I had the blessing of building a studio for the Lord on some land we had acquired. We had to tear down old existing structures to build the new. The Lord gave direction and instruction for the project, and I followed. After ten years, it needed some renovation and restructuring. I had given the building and the ministry of the church to my spiritual children, Francisco and Deserae Arboleda. It was now their ministry and building to steward, but they still desired me to have a place of honor as founder in their church and ministry. I have been extremely blessed by their love, and I deeply care for them.

Together, we conferred regarding the renovations and decor to the building and soon discovered that our perceptions were very different in some of the areas requiring updates. Some of it included matters of simple decorating preferences. We all loved decorating and had all personally achieved great outcomes over the years, but our tastes were different. At times you could feel a slight tension in the air that none of us wanted. We wanted to love and respect each other well through the process, and we understood that it would take some clear and peaceful communication as we submitted our thoughts and preferences to each other.

I remember sitting down with them one day amid all the transition to share our hearts. We didn't want to hurt each other and were careful to respect each other's opinions and preferences. I understood that the final decisions were to be made by them and that I needed to prepare to relinquish and defer. They were willing to defer also, although they were not required to.

I am a strong leader by nature, and when I communicate personal preferences, I can be direct. I could feel their longing to please me but also their struggle to take ownership of the project and implement the direction and choices they were sensing. The Lord helped us all to maintain love, flexibility, and honor in the journey, and the upgrades turned out wonderful. Even though they did not need to do this, they submitted renovation and decorating decisions for my input, and I submitted my ideas to them. When we had a difference of opinion, we listened to each other's hearts on how we came to that choice and the reasoning behind it. It turned out to be a valuable journey for all of us as we embraced the process and embraced and honored each other. In the end, we had a stronger bond and celebrated the outcome together. Although this was a small, natural situation, it enabled us to pass the tests we walked through and established increased love, appreciation, and trust for one another.

I was in my own spiritual transition season at that time, learning how to transition from being the lead visionary of the church and the founder and director of media vision and activities in the studio. Because I had given those ministries to Francisco and Deserae, I now had to learn how to stand back and let them increase in visible leadership as I decreased. I will always be their spiritual mother filled with God's maternal love and care for them, but my new role in the church was to be that of an encourager, mentor, and one to come alongside and empower. I have appreciated and cherished the patience, love, and honor, they graciously granted me as I transitioned into my new season. My transition in this season, although not flawless, has been successful and peaceful due to open processing with each other in love. They have been wonderful as we have transitioned together. I am truly blessed.

Generations that run together must embrace process that is at times uncomfortable. This is part of turning our hearts to each other.

Willingness to Pick Up the Pieces

Years ago, I received what I believed was a direction from the Lord. I submitted it to my team, and they had concerns and did not feel at peace signing off on it. I have always believed that we could be in complete unity as a team, so I was committed to not moving ahead until we were in agreement. I listened to their concerns and went back to prayer but continued to feel to move in the direction He had given me. I approached the team again and shared the following: "I feel this direction is from the Lord, but I want to respect your concerns. Can I ask you one question? If I were to move forward in this direction in faith and obedience and it fails, would you be willing to support me and help me pick up the pieces?" They were silent for a moment and then one by one said, "Yes, I will be there for you, and we will pick up the pieces together if needed."

That was the unity I needed to move forward. I fulfilled the direction the Lord issued on that assignment, and praise the Lord, there were no pieces to pick up.

Since that time, I have had a few opportunities to share this with younger generation leaders when they have wanted to pursue a specific direction they believed was from the Lord. It is important that we celebrate those who are eager to take leaps of faith. I have noticed many in the younger generation willing to take risks. Of course, wisdom is needed in the decision-making process, but if they truly feel a direction is from the Lord, are we as older generation leaders willing to run with them ... and if needed, lovingly help them to pick up the pieces on any failure,

> **If they truly feel a direction is from the Lord, are we as older generation leaders willing to run with them ... and if needed, lovingly help them to pick up the pieces on any failure, without judgment or disdain?**

without judgment or disdain? You need to be honest with the concerns in your spirit, and you need to be clear as to how you will run with them. Perhaps it is only in prayer.

I was approached by a next-generation leader, whom I have cheered on with a "mother's heart" for many years. He was stepping into a large building acquisition. I had concerns in my spirit for him and voiced them in a way that would not dampen his faith, but I felt that I needed to submit my spiritual sense. He was able to acquire the building, and I celebrated with him but continued to carry him and the building in prayer.

Over time, the building turned out to be a burden with numerous spiritual attacks on his ministry as a result. I engaged in fervent intercession and warfare for him and remained his cheerleader. I prayed for the Lord to sustain him and grant him wisdom during the painful season.

Without going into details, he grew in wisdom and insight through warfare and loss. His message, ministry opportunities, and anointing increased, and God worked everything together for his good. He took the risk of faith, and even though there were some pieces to pick up, heaven celebrated his risk and willingness to love and serve his God.

Let's celebrate faith and not abandon each other if things don't turn out the way they were expected to. Stand with and for each other.

Battles Don't Mean It Is Over

Every relationship can suffer hardship, but that doesn't mean it is time to pack up or change direction. In most cases, things can be worked out, and of course, relational conflicts need to be resolved. The enemy would love to drive wedges between the generations as this would ensure a victory for him. We must fight for each other and not against each other.

One of the greatest demonic culprits involved in warfare between the generations is the spirit of Leviathan. Leviathan is referred to in scripture as the "twisted serpent" (Isaiah 27:1), and I have discerned and observed this spirit in action repeatedly. It twists communications in such a way that what is being spoken isn't always what is heard. Misunderstandings and offenses come as a result, causing great pain in many, who then believe the relationship is over.

Leviathan is also referred to as "the king of the sons of pride" (Job 41:34). When under the assault of this spirit, it is important to invite the Lord to reveal any landing strip of pride in your life that this spirit might use as a legal entry point. In conflicts and tensions, usually pride is lurking on some level. Something that has helped me when I have battled Leviathan is to pray fervently for the one(s) who are opposing me. I engage in warfare on their behalf and pray for blessings to fill them. It is not always easy to pray those prayers, but they change my heart and position me for breakthrough.

When relationships are attacked, the enemy has a bigger agenda than your situation—he wants to destroy generational unity. You might need some time to heal before you can process well, and you might need a third party to mediate, but don't quit unless it's absolutely necessary.

We are promised victory in the battle (2 Corinthians 2:14), so let's commit to winning.

Unoffendable Love

Offense is deadly, and it is the breeding ground for all kinds of sinful violations that destroy relationship. In every offense, there are five transgressions that are activated: anger, bitterness, judgment, unforgiveness, and pride. Each one harms relationships, invites warfare, and bears personal consequence. Making a commitment to be unoffendable will help safeguard our relationships with one another. Speak the truth in love, for sure. Confront with grace when necessary, but refuse to take offense. Offense in the heart only destroys and does not build or offer healing. I highly recommend my book, *Live Unoffendable,* and my study guide, *Unoffendable Love* (which includes video and audio teachings of each lesson).[5] When you are tempted with offense, turn your attention to look for something good. Gather the nuggets that are hiding in the situation for you to discover and discern the growth opportunities.

---

5 See resource offered at back of book

Remember that no one is perfect. You are not perfect, and neither is the one you are building relationship with. Your imperfections can potentially irritate or hurt each other. When they do, be quick to forgive and cover each other. Don't hold a grudge and allow your heart to become bitter. Offense is a killer, but unoffendable love creates life.

Create Opportunity

Building a relationship takes time and intentionality. If there is no connection, a relationship cannot grow. You can have a bag of carrot seeds in your cupboard, but if you do not connect them to the soil, they will only be carrot seeds and never carrots. They have the potential to be carrots, but they must be planted, watered, exposed to light, and nurtured in order to grow. Relationships are the same. They require connection and nurture.

I personally build my closest relationships while working on ministry projects together and serving alongside one another. I particularly love working with younger generation leaders on assignments and events because it offers great opportunities to connect heart-to-heart. When we labor together, we come to know and love each other in expanded ways.

Hearts connect quickly when you spend time praying or worshipping together. Our church hosts daily prayer meetings, and those who regularly attend bond. Often after the prayer meeting, a few of us go out together for something to eat and to enjoy fellowship. The bonding continues.

Many of the next-generation leaders that the Lord has connected me with are scattered across the nation(s). What has helped tremendously are online "zoom" gatherings where we can be together for a time of sharing with one another for an hour or so. I have had to be deliberate in building these times together because life is full of time-grabbers.

I also enjoy lunch engagements at a restaurant or hosting the next generation for times of gathering and fellowship in my home. Sometimes these are spiritual gatherings and other times for fun and fellowship. I also enjoy going shopping together, taking walks, or doing a chore together.

Be intentional and plan to invest time into building relationships intergenerationally.

CONVERSATION POINT

Discuss the importance of processing through differences in order to grow in love, honor, and respect.

ACTIVATION

Identify any specific areas of conflict you have faced with those of the older or younger generation. Pray into the situation and ask the Lord for wisdom on how to secure a victory.

Chapter Nine

QUESTIONS AND RESPONSES
Patricia King and Benjamin Deitrick

Can I identify more than one spiritual father or mother in my life?

Patricia King: Various leaders could answer this question differently, and I respect everyone's input and perspective. However, I come from believing that we have one Father (who is in heaven). He releases His parental nature and attributes through several ministers to represent His heart to His son or daughter, although some might identify one key individual as their primary spiritual father or mother. Not one person can manifest all the parental aspects of our Heavenly Father. One might demonstrate a specific quality of His fatherly or motherly attributes, and another minister will be seasoned in another characteristic.

I was having a conversation with a friend and explained my perspective to her in this way: "I sense and feel the Father's love for you. He adores you and wants you to experience His fatherly presence in your life and ministry. As a result, He has blessed several leaders in your life with His heart for you. He places "fathers and mothers" around you to represent various aspects of His parental nature and love. Some are more casual than others, but all represent specific facets of His heart. He wants you to discern Him in them and to embrace Him as your true Father and Mother. He desires you to honor the individuals He uses as you see His attributes displayed but to fully acknowledge Him, your heavenly Father, as the author and initiator."

Everyone has a spiritual Father and Mother—God. You will find Him manifesting His parental nature and function through many—some will be closer than others to you and others might be very obscure.

Benjamin Deitrick: 1 Corinthians 4:15 says, "For though you might have ten thousand instructors in Christ, yet you do not have many fathers; for in Christ Jesus I have begotten you through the gospel."

The word used for "many" in the phrase "not many Fathers" is the word *polus* (phonetic: pol-oos'). It means "much, many, often." In other words, Paul is saying you don't have many (quantity) genuine spiritual parents and they do not come that often.

It also doesn't say you only have one (singular) spiritual parent throughout the course of your life, other than God—the constant Father of our souls, as I have already shared.

Genuine spiritual parents are rare and precious, and we are to thank God for them in the seasons they parent us and love and honor them always.

Can I be both a spiritual parent and a spiritual son or daughter?

Benjamin Deitrick: The answer is yes. The Bible describes an amazing relationship between Timothy and Paul. Paul met Timothy during his second missionary journey, and historians tell us he had a Jewish mother who became a Christian and a Greek father. Timothy is described as a spiritual son of Paul, while Paul identifies himself as Timothy's father in the Lord (1 Timothy 1:2). This question is perfectly personified in the life of Timothy.

He was a son of Paul, dearly loved, but he was also a spiritual father. He was entrusted with a massive leadership role in the city of Ephesus and the church there. In fact, history tells us that Timothy was the first Christian Bishop of Ephesus and lived until around 97 AD.

We need three different connections in our lives once we have come to a basic level of maturity in our Christian walk. We need a Paul, a Timothy, and a Barnabas. Paul is the one who is teaching and parenting us, Timothy is one we are parenting, mentoring, or pouring into, and Barnabas is a peer who we encourage and who encourages us. For our purposes, let's briefly look at the first two examples.

We all need parenting and mentoring. God is our Father and truly, when it is all boiled down, He is all we need. But we are called to walk in relationship in life and in the Body of Christ. God will appoint individuals who will carry His anointing of Fatherhood to impart to us. It is always a joy and gift to be parented and mentored, taught, trained, and enlarged by one who is more mature in the Lord. This is the "Paul" we can be blessed by.

We can't remain in a state of only receiving our whole life and be well-rounded and mature. We need to be giving and making disciples, who then make disciples who, in turn, make more disciples. This is the call of the Great Commission! The five steps of leadership are often described as:

I do, you watch. I do, you help. You do, I help. You do, I watch. You do, someone else watches.

We can see from this simple, powerful example that in the maturing process, we eventually go from the student to the teacher.

You will always have a heart of love, respect, and honor for your spiritual parent(s), but you eventually mature to become a parent yourself. The seasons of parenting and being parented often overlap and happen simultaneously. This has been true in my own life countless times.

If I have never had an official spiritual parent myself, can I be a spiritual parent?

Patricia King: Absolutely. God is your spiritual parent, so you have the best One ever. I never had official spiritual parents in human form in my life, but I am a spiritual parent.

Can I expect a spiritual parent to open doors of opportunity for me?

Patricia King: The answer is yes; that is in the heart of a spiritual parent … but there are considerations. Robert Hotchkin, founder of Robert Hotchkin Ministries (and my dear spiritual son) shares the following story that gives a great answer to your question.

Robert Hotchkin:
Many years ago I was ministering at an event hosted by a pastor who was a couple of years into leading his church. After the conference wrapped up, we met in his office where he shared how his congregation and ministry were not growing as quickly as he had expected them to, and he thought that what he needed was a spiritual father. He asked me if I would be willing to play that role in his life. I was surprised by the request as we really didn't know each other yet. I let him know I was honored that he would think of me as having the potential to be a spiritual father for him. But since I didn't know him well, and because we lived so far apart, I asked what his expectations were.

My experience of having a spiritual parent was that you spent time together, worked together, built together, and to a great degree, "did life" together—just like an actual child does with an actual parent. That way, spiritual parents get to really see the strengths, weaknesses, gifts, and callings of the one they are "parenting," so they can help him or her grow in areas of strength and deal with any areas of weakness. I let this pastor know that this was my experience of having been wonderfully spiritually parented, and I was open to trying to figure out a way how to make that happen in the midst of my busy schedule and a significant geographic distance, which would make frequent time together a bit more challenging

He explained that all he really wanted from a spiritual father was someone who would open doors for him. He was simply looking for someone who could connect him with publishers, media opportunities, and conference invitations. He thought if he had a higher profile, his ministry and congregation would grow faster. I let him know that once I got to know him better, I would be open to serving him in those areas, but that *I really didn't think he wanted a spiritual father nearly so much as he wanted a publicist or promoter.*

My experience of having been very well spiritually parented was that yes, indeed, there were times my spiritual mother helped open a door for me, but what she had really done (and still does) was to help me walk through any door that *did* open as a better representative and re-presenter of Jesus and His Kingdom.

I let this minister know that I thought the only way we could really build that type of spiritual relationship, connection, and trust, would be to spend time together whenever possible in person, on the phone, and online. After all, our One True Spiritual Parent, Heavenly Father, has brought us back through His Son into what we lost in the Garden—the ability to spend time with Him. He wants to walk and talk with us every day to help us grow in our ability to operate as His dominion stewards, Kingdom agents of impact, and most of all, as His sons and daughters. Spiritual mothers and fathers in our lives do the same.

What are some practical ways I can spiritually parent someone?

Patricia King: Here are a few ways that will help give you vision for ways you can serve your spiritual children.

1. **Pray** for those you are spiritually parenting. This will not only offer them covering but will connect you to the Father's heart for them.

2. **Decree** the Word and promises of God over them. The Word does not return void. A decree is an official, authoritative declaration sourced in God. This is different from prayer (requesting on their behalf), this is like prophesying over them. Decrees fulfill what they are called to achieve (Isaiah 55:11).

3. **Connect** to encourage and build relationship. It only takes a moment to send a text or email to connect and offer encouragement. Follow up with them regarding things they have shared. Call them and have heart-to-hearts on the phone or on online platforms. When possible, take time to connect in person for casual visits, deep conversations, or fun and fellowship.

4. **Partner** with their projects, interests, and assignments when possible. Your interest and support will mean a lot. Partnering can include financial partnership and also your physical involvement in their assignments when they are comfortable with that.

5. **Coach.** Submit wisdom, counsel, and growth elements to them when applicable. This includes offering them keys from your experience or specific resources to empower acceleration in their calling.

6. **Bring confrontation and correction** when needed. You do not want your spiritual children to continue in error or misbehavior. If you love them, you will help them get back on track.

7. **Process challenging and painful situations that they are walking through.** Be a listening ear. Help them to receive the healing and breakthrough they need. Follow up until they are at peace.

8. **Defend them** in conflict. Walk with them through their battles, covering them, believing in them.

9. **Do life with them** when possible. In cases where you have proximity and relationship, you might want to invite them to join you in the activities of life. For example, you can go shopping with them, make dinner together, fix cars, assemble items together, build memories with them through special events, trips, or vacations, and go on ministry trips together.

10. **Co-lead an assignment or project.** Build something together where you are both involved in leading a project or assignment. Delegate the areas of responsibility and build together.

Trust is an issue for me. Is trust important in the relationship between spiritual parents and children?

Benjamin Deitrick: The book *Right Relationship,* by Tom Marshall, has changed my life as I've read it many times over the years. Tom goes over the basic building blocks of relationships. He hypothesizes that there are four main elements: love, trust, understanding, and honor. He describes all of them, but the one that most impacted me was trust.

He said trust was the one that took the longest to build…and was also the most fragile. It can take 20 years to build real trust in a relationship, and it can be destroyed in a matter of minutes with harsh words, actions, or abuse. In the time we live in, trust is a huge issue. It is a huge issue because of the amount of pain, trauma, and heartache most people have experienced along the lines of broken relationships. If we take that brokenness into a spiritual parent/child relationship, it can impact the relationship in many negative ways.

It can be hard for a spiritual parent to trust a spiritual child if they have been hurt and vice versa. Walls begin to form, and the entire relational dynamic becomes counterproductive. That is why I would encourage every spiritual parent to be as attentive as they can to their own areas of weakness and engage in inner healing, deliverance, and overall health of soul before entering into a spiritual parenting relationship. I say this especially to the spiritual parent because you are the one who is mostly giving in this dynamic, and the spiritual child is the one who is mostly receiving.

Often, it is in the dynamic of spiritual parenting that a spiritual child receives much inner healing and health of soul, but that certainly doesn't mean they shouldn't also try to enter the relationship as healed as possible to be able to receive as much as possible.

If there is to be a true impartation of life, both the spiritual child and the spiritual parent must be open and express a certain amount of vulnerability. Every relationship has a certain amount of risk involved in it because of the nature of fallen people, and if the dynamic of spiritual parent/child is to work, that risk must be taken. The risk predicates vulnerability and trust, which results in a godly depth and intimacy.

Having said this, no spiritual parent or spiritual child is perfect —there never has been and never will be! Our trust in a spiritual parent or child is based mainly on our trust in the Lord. We entrust ourselves fully and completely to God and then choose to trust, walk with, believe in, and give grace to those with whom He calls us into a relationship.

Even Jesus did not entrust Himself to any person, but only to God. John 2:24 says, "But Jesus would not entrust himself to them, for he knew all people." Jesus knew the fallen nature of man. He entrusted Himself to God and loved others perfectly. He did not naively ignore the fallen nature of man, nor was He shocked by it.

We are often shocked by the sins and shortcomings of others, but that is nonsensical. Should we be more shocked by others' sins than our own? God is the only one who is perfect, but that doesn't mean we can't trust people or have relationships with them.

God is the One who is fathering us—He is perfect. In His fathering, He brings imperfect people into our lives to represent aspects of Himself. Many times people say, "I will trust someone if they prove themselves." I can understand that and there is, of course, a good point to that, but sometimes we don't realize that when we say "trust," what we really mean is that we are looking for someone to be perfect.

If you are called to be a spiritual parent, your spiritual child will not be perfect. Trust God in them and cover their shortcomings.

If you are a spiritual child, your spiritual father or mother will not be perfect. They will make mistakes. Give grace and trust God to be everything you need—even when they fail.

How do I know when and how to initiate boundaries when I feel I am being expected to constantly give but it is not reciprocated?

Patricia King: Love requires freedom to give in order to fully function as love. Love cannot be taken; it must be given freely. If you are sensing pressure to give, but your heart is not free to give, then this needs to be addressed. Sometimes the pressure comes from yourself because of unrealistic expectations, and sometimes it originates from others.

When you feel pressure, go to God, and ask Him where the pressure is coming from. If it is self-originated, then ask Him to reveal the source of the expectation. The answer could be simple or complex, but once you see clearly, then position yourself before Him to receive freedom from pressure. Ask Him to give you a heart that is fully released to give freely. If you need someone to minister to you, then don't delay. Get the help you need. When you think, "I have to" rather than "I get to," then it is a sign to deal with the pressure.

If the pressure is external and coming from another person, in most cases you will need to communicate with them directly. With a desire to help them understand a better way to relate, you can unpack the dynamics with them. Do not come from a place of offense but from genuine love for them. If they get defensive, keep your peace. Clearly communicate your boundaries and ensure that they understand.

Other times there is no need for an actual confrontation but simply communicate the changes you want. For example, let's say they call you late into the night and demand your time and attention numerous times in a week. Simply inform them kindly that you are not available to take calls after 7:00 p.m. (or whatever time you want to set) and that you will be open for no more than two or three connections in a week due to your schedule.

How do I handle feeling rejected or looked over by spiritual parents who are reaching out to others, but I feel invisible to them? Others are receiving what I believe I should be getting.

Patricia King: I feel compassion for any who feel left out, passed over, or rejected. Everyone is so valued in God's eyes, and He wants you to feel secure and loved.

That being said, the best solution ever is to die—die to self. A dead man does not feel rejection or jealousy. Jesus said to take up our cross daily because He knew we would need to. Sometimes we need to speak out loud in His presence, "Jesus, I die to my need to be acknowledged and blessed by others." That way, it moves Jesus right into position to be everything you need. By faith, receive all you need from Him and tell Him that you trust Him. Feel free to also ask Him for any help He wants you to have and see what happens.

A great way to overcome covetousness or jealousy is to bless and celebrate those who have what you desire, and ask God to even give them more. It breaks a stronghold in you and frees you to soar.

You attract to yourself what you believe. If you believe you are not getting what you need, then you won't—this is God's law of attraction. "Beloved, I pray that you may prosper in all things and be in health, just *as your soul prospers*" (3 John 1:2).

Believe the truth—you are God's cherished child, and He will give you everything you need. He will withhold no good thing from you.

CONVERSATION POINT

Add your own thoughts to each question and response in this section.

Chapter 10

♡

THE JOYS OF BEING A SPIRITUAL FATHER, MOTHER, SON, OR DAUGHTER

By numerous contributors

The following include experiences individuals have enjoyed in being spiritual fathers, mothers, sons, and daughters.

Dr. Brian Simmons, *Author of The Passion Translation:*

"True spiritual fathers continuously put the welfare of their sons and daughters first."

To raise up spiritual sons and daughters has been the greatest joy of my ministry! They soar higher than I, and I am proud of them. I love seeing others avoid some of the pitfalls of pride that hindered me in my journey. This generation is hungry for those who will prioritize their spiritual growth above our own accomplishments. True spiritual fathers continuously put the welfare of their sons and daughters first. They become the priority; we are not living for what they may bring to us. When their children achieve success, they are not envious; rather, they are ecstatic.

It is common for a parent to want their kids to be better than them in every aspect. Brothers compete, fathers do not. So I have been delighted to see my "kids" write books, plant churches, and influence people around the world. Truly, I could echo the testimony of the Apostle John when he writes: "It is the greatest joy of my life to hear that my children are consistently living their lives in the ways of truth!" (3 John 4).

Pastor Peter Rosselle, *Senior Pastor of King of Kings Worship Center*:

"I have chosen to 'gladly spend and be spent'…"

In our ministry, the Father has brought dozens of younger men and women; some far from God, some seeking closer, authentic relationships with the Father, Son, and Holy Spirit. He has also blessed us with seasoned leaders willing to mentor and disciple believers of every generation.

My assignment has never been clearer. It is my responsibility (and privilege), to turn my heart to the next generation. Paul says in 2 Corinthians 12:14-15, "I will not be burdensome to you; for I do not seek yours, but you. For the children ought not to lay up for the parents, but the parents for the children. And I will very gladly spend and be spent for your souls."

I too have chosen to "gladly spend and be spent" to pass on the timeless truths of God's Kingdom rule in the earth.

Pastor Patricia Rosselle, *Co-Pastor of King of Kings Worship Center:*

"As a spiritual mother, I am called to ...create opportunities that help others soar."

It is a privilege and an honor to be a spiritual mother, called to invest in the destiny and dreams of spiritual sons and daughters the Lord has entrusted to me. Building trust and authentic relationship opens the door to becoming a part of their lives where speaking truth in love is welcome. I believe that feedback is a gift, and I am intentional about providing both positive and corrective feedback to help people grow into the mature warriors God has called them to be. The word tells us that our gifts will make room for us. As a spiritual mother, I am called to help make room by creating opportunities that help others soar to new heights in their walk in the Lord.

Dr. Michelle Burkett, *Founder of Michelle Burkett Ministries*:

"My natural parents were also my spiritual parents."

I grew up in a ministry family. Before I was a year old, my mother read the entire Bible to me, setting in place the Word as the foundation of my life. In the mornings, my father would prepare my breakfast before school and, as I ate, he would read to me from the Gospels. As I grew, God's Word was made alive to me as I saw Truth in action through my ministry parents.

I watched my dad cut and deliver wood to those who needed it or answer many a crisis call at inopportune moments, and I learned that ministry is a life laid down before God and poured out to others—willingly and lovingly. I learned that God is always enough as my parents would give from what little we had, and God would return it with MORE. I saw the reality of God's power as people were healed or delivered. I experienced God's protection because of my praying parents. Seeing Mom and Dad walk through both the hard and the good, I learned that God's Word is LIFE; I learned how to breathe that Life and make it my own. I gleaned a thankful heart, strength, and absolute confidence in the Lord. Even through the worst of times, my mother always said she had a song of Joy in her heart… A "tune" that was taught to me well.

Dave and Royree Jensen, *Missionaries to Bougainville:*

From Rambo to Statesman

There stood Ishmael, machete in hand; tall, strong, and very black. His dreadlocks making a declaration of his independent spirit. He typified his people group. Ishmael was a young man who had led a revolutionary army against his government and the mining giants who had raped the land and stolen from his people. He had the smell of justice in his nostrils.

Bougainville, a small island in the Pacific Ocean, had been struggling for independence in an ocean of negative political voices and the greedy conglomerates, groping for the God-given wealth on this island.

As ministers of the gospel and spiritual parents to a nation, it has been our privilege to walk with Ishmael for 25 years as he grew into a man of faith. We witnessed his development from a

'Rambo' to a 'Statesman' through the power of the gospel, prayer, and the moving of the Spirit. We sat together often and talked of his plans to one day bring his nation to full independence and godliness.

Some weeks ago we were in Bougainville again, walking into the Presidential residence. President Ishmael Toroama was there to greet us, dressed in a suit fit for a king.

A nation on the verge of redemption.

Ben and Jodie Hughes, *Founders of Pour It Out Ministries*:

> *"Being a spiritual parent isn't a 'checklist,' it's a love journey!"*

We recall a challenging season of ministry when it seemed everything was crashing in around us and were struggling to keep our heads above water. We needed help to navigate one of those ministry challenges, and seasons of attacks that threatened to break us. We'll never forget sitting in the kitchen of a true spiritual father and humbly (and with lots of trepidation) looking him in the eye and simply asking, "Will you help us?"

His immediate "yes" was soothing, but he didn't just give us wisdom, he held us close with present love and "boots on the ground" encouragement as we walked through a minefield of "swirly crazy." His concern for our hearts, and not just our ministry, helped us process well and kept us moving forward, going beyond "the valley of the shadow" into fresh, clear water.

In a recent pioneering ministry endeavor that took scary faith (like jumping out of a plane and building the parachute on the way down kind of faith), a spiritual mother truly championed us. But it was always more than words, it was her present love that became like fuel—she showed up to walk with us through the journey! Because she was "with" us, we felt like "anything was possible." Her faith in us propelled us beyond the ceiling of our last breakthrough, into what hadn't been walked in before. That marked us.

A hallmark of the spiritual parents in our lives has been their ability to champion us, call us higher, and love us through the barrage of enemy fire, or the very real challenging stuff of life and ministry.

Being a spiritual parent isn't a "checklist," it's a love journey. We've been personally moved by the selfless love of spiritual parents in our lives to love us into "the more"… and that's a great descriptor of a mum and dad in the faith.

Paul and Kim Owens, *Senior Pastors of Fresh Start Church*:

"Sometimes the responsibility can be weighty…"

The greatest joy and reward is seeing the mantle that God has given you reproduced and flourishing greater in the one(s) in whom you've invested. While sometimes the responsibility can be weighty, in the end, it bears great fruit as they continue to carry on the mantle. Speaking the truth in love, accountability, and spiritual discipleship, require focus, patience, and commitment to obtain the best possible outcome in your spiritual son or daughter.

As you share life experiences, you guard and guide them through the ups and downs. Your goal is to help build strong spiritual shoulders that will hold up under the weight of every spiritual and natural challenge and task. We have learned that it's very important to know what it means to be a son and not a servant. A servant serves from a motive to get something, a son serves out of love and loyalty for the mantle that you carry. The end result for the son is the passing of a mantle that he/she has already sacrificed for. Both the parent and the spiritual son or daughter share the reward of a mantle kept in motion for the next generation.

Katherine Ruonala, *Senior Leader Glory City Church*:

> *"Our ceiling should be the floor from which the next generation can be launched."*

One of the greatest joys in my life is to see spiritual sons and daughters rise and excel in their callings. It has always been my belief that our ceiling should be the floor from which the next generations can be launched. Sadly, in some church models, when a ministry within a church begins to grow, they can be considered a threat, and if they are more gifted or have more favor than the senior leader, inevitably they need to leave the church to fulfill their destiny. But in healthy families, a parent's heart is to see their children fly higher than they ever could, and this is the heart posture of a true spiritual father or mother. I like to picture my connection to sons and daughters like a beautiful flower with big petals. Our churches and ministries could be seen as the center where our spiritual sons and daughters can connect to and be nourished and encouraged. They do not have to be contained within the center of the flower but celebrated and encouraged and mentored as beautiful petals that can grow and flourish while being safe to maintain connection and relationship with us.

True promotion is something only the Lord can do, and we are to continually point sons and daughters to the Lord as their source of everything. However, we can use our platforms and influence as a launching pad and encouragement to next-generation leaders. My experience has been that the more I share the opportunities and favor that the Lord gives me, the more opportunities and favor He brings me. Then the more successful your sons and daughter are, the bigger we all become—the Kingdom of God expands, the Lord is glorified, and the Gospel is preached. God wants His glory to cover the earth as the waters cover the sea, and that will happen as we encourage one another. We need each other to see this mission accomplished, and what a great privilege it is to champion the next generation of leaders. Their success is our success!

Pastor Michele Jackson, *Senior Pastor of Hope Christian Church:*

"I have experienced the joy and the heartbreak of spiritual parenting."

I have experienced the joy and the heartbreak of spiritual parenting; both spiritual abuse and spiritual enrichment and equipping. For healthy spiritual parenting to function, the eyes of our hearts must be opened by Holy Spirit to discern the portion of our inheritance that is accessible by the Spirit and which portion is housed in flesh and blood (Ephesians 1:17-22). I honor my late father Bishop Harry Jackson and Bishop Bill Hamon for modeling and teaching me how to surrender to the call of God, how to discern my portion, and how to walk in my mantle.

Earlier in my journey, as a teen, misplaced expectations mixed with wounded leaders created an environment where relationship inequities and disappointment abounded. Wounded by well-meaning leaders, offense caused the chasm that stunted both my relational and spiritual growth. As I cried out desperately to encounter the love of God, the Father poured out His Spirit upon me supernaturally in my prayer closet and through both of my spiritual dads. Cultivating desperation and hunger for God shifted my ability to discern my portion.

Malachi underscores that relational brokenness which requires a unique prophetic anointing to bring the Father's blessing; one that encompasses emotional healing, relational reconciliation, restitution, and wholeness. In fact, a messenger or prophet commissioned into this assignment by the Lord must carry this yoke (curse)-destroying anointing in order to abate the impending judgment of God. We must carry this same anointing to the generation rising next; teaching them to observe the things we have learned (Matthew 28:18-20).

Pastor Francisco Arboleda, *Senior Pastor of Shiloh Fellowship*:

"They had their work cut out for them but they never gave up."

I remember watching Billy Graham on TV as a young boy. He loved God and fearlessly spoke with passion. I often tried to imitate him and others in front of the mirror at night. I didn't realize that God was birthing something in me. I didn't want to be an athlete or superhero – I wanted to be like the heroes of the faith.

Later, I was blessed to have spiritual parents and mentors who saw the call of the Lord on my life. Honestly, they had their work cut out but never gave up. They believed in me. Through them, I was strengthened emotionally, intellectually, and spiritually. It was what I needed.

The Apostle Paul wrote to Timothy, *"For God has not given us a spirit of fear, but of power, love, and a sound mind."* He said "us." He included Timothy in the promise and made him a part of the story.

I am grateful to God for my spiritual parents and mentors. Because of them, I'm no longer just the boy looking in the mirror; I have become a part of the story. I'm walking in my calling with them. Together, we are a family set apart for the glory of the Lord.

Pastor Deserae Arboleda, *Co-pastor of Shiloh Fellowship:*

"...covered, championed, and course corrected..."

I remember when I entered into a new level of relationship with a leader who's a spiritual mother and mentor in my life. My husband and I were pioneering a new season in our lives and had stepped into full-time ministry. I had so many concerns about not measuring up to the task at hand. In the beginning of that season, the Lord gave me a dream that was repeated two years later.

Both dreams began with us waking from sleep in the morning, and to our surprise, our spiritual mother was sitting on the end of our bed. I was undone and frazzled on the inside, thinking, "Oh my gosh—my room is a wreck!" And it was, unusually so. I was completely embarrassed in the dream and freaking out over what she must think. Without skipping a beat, she looked intentionally into our eyes with love. Her attention was fully on us, and not the mess in the room—or our immaturity or deficiency. She saw us as Jesus did, with the call and the purpose He had for us. She saw our future and loved us into it.

To this day, this is the love that we have been covered in, championed with, and yes, even "course corrected" in. It took trust on our part and hers. She loved, trusted, and released us into opportunity and responsibility, and we trusted her love. She wanted us to succeed even more than we wanted to succeed (like a good mom). Intentionality and vulnerability allow love to truly happen. When the generations run together in this love, trust, vulnerability, and intentionality, we change history and shape our future into Kingdom culture.

Pastor Dustin Williams, *Associate Pastor Shiloh Fellowship*:

> ***"We would not have lasted in ministry if it were not for him…"***

Several years ago I faced a medical issue called "Bell's palsy" that caused the left side of my face to become paralyzed. It was so severe that I couldn't close my left eye, smile, or talk without slobbering uncontrollably. As a pastor, speaking is a major part of what I do, and I had resigned myself to the reality that my ministry was over. I had no idea how I could ever stand behind a pulpit and preach in that condition. I remember sitting down with my lead pastor, who was also my spiritual father, and with tears in my eyes I let him know that I was resigning. He looked at me and said, "That's not going to work because I am having you preach this Sunday." I was shocked and said, "But I can't even talk." He replied with words I will never forget, "I can understand you just fine." That Sunday I preached to our congregation of over 1,200 people one of the most powerful messages I have ever preached. He believed in me and the call of God on my life. He was willing to fight for that call on my life when I couldn't. He taught me the importance of pushing through when it's hard and inconvenient. My wife and I would not have lasted in ministry if it were not for him. He showed me the importance of encouraging the next generation to fight for the call of God on their lives.

Pastor Heather Williams, *Administration Pastor of Shiloh Webchurch*:

> *"Being a spiritual parent is far more than just a fancy title or a new trend to jump on..."*

There was a season in our ministry when it seemed that many of our leaders were going through an incredibly tumultuous season. I remember one specific Sunday morning about five minutes before the service was about to start when a leader came up to me crying. With tears running down her cheeks, she told me that she was going through a very difficult personal struggle. No sin was involved, but she felt she needed to step down because she wasn't good enough to lead in ministry any longer. I remember my eyes welling with tears, and a deep compassion I had never known came over me. I told her that there was no way I was going to let her suffer alone and in silence, and that I would not let her step away from me or the team for that matter. She fell into my arms and began to sob uncontrollably. It was in that moment that I had a deep realization that being a spiritual parent is far more than just a fancy title or a new trend to jump on. It is the willingness to stay in the relationship, even when it's hard. It's fighting for people when they can't fight or stand on their own. Being a spiritual parent is not only an honor, but it is a high calling. The role of a spiritual parent is not to be taken lightly, but instead, it is something to be valued, taken care of, and honored.

CONVERSATION POINT

Share your joys and experiences. Comment on any of the testimonies that moved your heart.

ACTIVATION

Write in a journal some of your fond memories of parenting or being parented in your spiritual journey.

Chapter 11

THERE IS HEALING IN HIS WINGS
Patricia King

> But for you who fear My name, the sun of righteousness will rise with healing in its wings; and you will go forth and skip about like calves from the stall.
>
> You will tread down the wicked, for they will be ashes under the soles of your feet on the days which I am preparing, says the LORD of hosts. – *Malachi 4:2*

It is possible that you just finished reading the previous chapter that contains many expressions of joy and gratitude from spiritual parents and children, and you are feeling regret, sadness, or even anger. You do not relate to having spiritual parents in your life who cared for your growth and welfare. Or you might have experienced damaging interactions with those who were leaders or spiritual parents in your life. Maybe you feel rejected, abandoned, or mistreated. Or perhaps after reading the accounts, you recall the pain of having your spiritual children whom you loved deeply and cared for with all your heart, dishonor, forsake, or rebel against you.

These are very real scenarios for many. The Bible is full of such accounts. I think of David being forsaken by his mother and father and then later, the pain he experienced through the actions and loss of his son, Absalom (2 Samuel 19:5). I think of Noah, who was dishonored by his youngest son Ham (Genesis 9:22-25), or Paul weeping over those he had discipled who became enemies of the cross (Philippians 3:18). Then there's Jesus as He lamented over Jerusalem (Matthew 23:37-39). You are not alone.

Often, when we are hurt, taken advantage of, or neglected, we respond with offense, bitter anger, and unforgiveness. This will only lock in the pain. Jesus wants to heal you. He IS the "Sun of righteousness," and His rays of healing will reach into every affected part of your soul. Invite Him to come into those areas and heal. The following are some keys that will help you experience freedom.

1. Identify the pain and its source.

Denial does not make the pain go away. A man was experiencing pain in his abdomen for several months but continued with his regular routine, ignoring the symptoms. The symptoms did not disappear—they worsened. His wife noticed that he was uncomfortable, but he told her it wasn't anything to be concerned about and refused medical attention for several more months. He finally made an appointment with the doctor who ordered various tests to determine the source of the pain. The reports came back to confirm a diagnosis of rapid-spreading, aggressive cancer. Unfortunately, because he failed to respond to the pain in the early stages, cancer filled his body with no option for treatment left. He passed within eight weeks. If he had been treated early, they could have successfully treated the condition.

Your pain is worthy to be addressed. God wants to identify the source of it and heal you of every ill effect.

Invite the Holy Spirit to reveal your pain and the source. If you need the help of a counselor, then seek the Lord for His direction on whom to approach.

2. Forgive.

When you identify the wrongdoings that created the pain, forgive the transgressor. Jesus declared on the cross, "Father, forgive them, for they know not what they do." None of us had repented from our sins… Yet, He forgave us. The one(s) who hurt you might never make things right, but you can forgive from the heart—and you need to. Forgiveness is not an option. Unforgiveness permanently fastens the pain and damage of the transgression to your soul. It can spread into your physical body, into relationships, and into your spiritual life. Unforgiveness is lethal.

Sometimes you will lack the feeling of forgiveness, but you can still make the willing choice to forgive, and as you continue to choose forgiveness, eventually the feelings will come.

In a ministry session once, a woman who had been sexually abused refused to forgive her perpetrator. She said, "I'm not letting him off the hook!" My response was, "But it's about getting his hook out of you." That is what forgiveness does.

We have been forgiven of ALL our sins when we accept Christ. We are commanded to forgive others who sin against us.

3. Receive healing by faith.

Jesus taught us: "Therefore I say to you, all things for which you pray and ask, believe that you have received them, and they will be granted you" (Mark 11:24).

The key in this passage is to receive WHEN you pray; not to wait until you experience results. Faith is heaven's currency, and through faith we engage in Kingdom transactions. Jesus paid for your healing two thousand years ago. It is available for you. Receive it by faith. The moment you do, it will begin to work in your life.

When you take vitamins or herbal supplements to correct a malfunction in your body, the moment you begin the therapy, the vitamins are at work. You might not notice results for a while, but they are already at work. It is the same with receiving by faith.

"Faith is the substance of things hoped for, it is the evidence of things not seen" (Hebrews 11:1).

Believe and receive. Whenever you feel the pain surface, position yourself to receive again. Eventually, the pain will leave and you will know freedom. Don't be discouraged if it takes a while. You are in a healing process the moment you begin to receive. If you need someone to minister to you, then reach out as the Lord directs you. He wants you healed.

4. Fill the empty places with Father's love.

Where people have failed, hurt, or disappointed you, invite your Father in heaven to fill those places in your heart with His love. Look to Him afresh—He is everything you need, and He deeply loves you. Daily, drink of His love. I like to take deep breaths as I receive His love into my body, soul, and spirit by faith. Breathe in His love.

5. Be filled with the Spirit.

The Holy Spirit will empower you with wisdom, insight, discernment, and revelation for your future. The areas of your life that were once weak He makes strong. He gives you fresh, bold love and seals your life with His protection. He replaces the old painful memories with new perspectives. He leads and guides you on a new path that is full of glory and purpose. Don't look back!

Have You Caused Pain?

We have just looked at some healing keys that can be applied when you have been hurt, but what about when you are the one who has caused the pain? It is usually much easier to take ownership of the pain others have inflicted upon us than taking ownership of the pain we have caused. In fact, we are often blinded to the pain we have caused.

Jesus said, "You hypocrite, first take the log out of your own eye, and then you will see clearly to take the speck out of your brother's eye!" (Matthew 7:5)

Here are some keys to help you start the process.

1. Invite Holy Spirit to bring conviction.

One of the roles of the Holy Spirit is to convict us of "sin, righteousness, and judgment" (John 16:8). Invite Him to reveal to you any attitudes, thoughts, words, or actions you have engaged in that have been dishonoring, rebellious, unloving, harmful, or prideful toward spiritual parents or children. When He convicts you, don't try to justify it. Take ownership of it.

2. Hear the heart of the one who is hurt.

In any relational conflict, there are always at least two perspectives. We always think our perspective is the right one. Oftentimes, we do not realize that we have hurt another with our words and choices because we are more focused on how we have been hurt. If healing and reconciliation are going to come, then we must listen well to the one(s) we have hurt. That means we are not to jump in with defensive attitudes and words but truly listen to their perspective. It might not be what you believe is accurate, but it is real to them and worthy to be addressed.

Empathize with them. Put yourself in their shoes. After listening, let them know you are sorry for their pain. (Saying sorry does not apportion blame but simply empathizes with how they feel.)

If you have a different perspective, gently ask them questions to clarify. Then, ask the Lord how you can help them come into a greater understanding of the situation. Sometimes you will need a mediator to help keep the processing objective.

3. Repent and receive forgiveness.

To repent is to change your thinking about something, but it also refers to turning in another direction. As an older generation leader, I realize that my generation of Baby Boomers was responsible for much of the moral decline that we witness in our day. In our younger years, during the 1960s and 70s, we pushed for and celebrated sexual freedom outside of marriage. We also embraced New Age practices, fought for abortion rights, created a drug epidemic, and much more. When we fast-forward fifty to sixty years, we see the devastating fruit of our choices. Our generation needs to take ownership of this, receive forgiveness from the Lord, and ask forgiveness from others for our choices. I have done this on public platforms and in intercession before the Lord.

Also as individuals, we have most likely made choices that have hurt others in our lives (i.e. spiritual parents and children). When the Holy Spirit reveals this to you, ask the Lord to forgive you, and receive forgiveness by faith. If the one you have hurt is aware of the pain, then go to them and ask them to forgive you. This can be in person when possible or through a note or letter.

"If we confess our sins, He is faithful and righteous, so that He will forgive us our sins and cleanse us from all unrighteousness" (1 John 1:9).

4. Restitution

Is there any area that you need to make things right? Ask Holy Spirit and the one whom you hurt.

We see a heart of restitution in Zacchaeus.

But Zacchaeus stopped and said to the Lord, "Behold, Lord, half of my possessions I am giving to the poor, and if I have extorted anything from anyone, I am giving back four times as much" (Luke 19:8).

5. Move forward on a new path

Learn lessons from your failures and mistakes, and then move forward. Do not be weighed down with guilt or self-condemnation. You are not defined by the mistakes of your past.

Do not call to mind the former things, or consider things of the past. Behold, I am going to do something new, now it will spring up; will you not be aware of it? I will even make a roadway in the wilderness, rivers in the desert (Isaiah 43:18,19).

It is time to rejoice in the goodness of God, and it is also time to "make the devil sorry he ever tried!" Invite the Holy Spirit to lead and guide you in His peace. You will have a renewed confidence to crush the lies of the enemy and to embrace the full plan of God for your life.

The enemy has attempted to destroy the love, unity, and partnership between the generations, but you will be used to crush his attempts and restore God's original plan. Are you ready to be a voice for Him? The hearts of the fathers will turn to the children and the children to the fathers.

CONVERSATION POINT

Discuss the importance of dealing with pain related to failed areas of relationship between the generations.

ACTIVATION

1. Search your heart for any way you have hurt a spiritual parent or child. Go through the key points in this chapter to make the wrongs right.
2. Identify areas where a spiritual parent or child has hurt you. Review the key points above and receive healing.

CONCLUDING REMARKS
Patricia King

The turning of the hearts of the fathers to the children and the children to the fathers is unto something. As Benjamin Deitrick shared in the introduction, the spirit and power of Elijah will be manifest through one company of people and not merely one person as was the case with Elijah and John the Baptist. But what is this call unto?

Elijah was a voice of confrontation, addressing the idolatry of his day, so that hearts would turn back to the Lord and declare that He is God. John the Baptist was a voice crying in the wilderness to prepare the way of the Lord. He turned sinners to the Lord and confronted religious lies and piety. In this hour, what is the purpose of one company giving voice to the Lord's will? It is again to prepare the way of the Lord but also to prepare the Bride of Christ.

While I was before the Lord over a two-day period (December 15–16 2022), the following prophetic understanding came through the Spirit of God. It was a sobering word and left me with a sense of awe and urgency in this hour. I believe the excerpts of that word shared below will give some concluding context for the purpose of *Hearts that Turn*.

Prepare the Way

Prepare the way of the Lord! ... I am offering a path of glory and blessing for all who desire to cleave to Me wholly in this hour.

Remove every stumbling block and crush every idol of the soul.

For I am coming soon for a people whose hearts are completely Mine.

I am looking for those who have fully surrendered to Me.

Today, I am calling the generations to run together to proclaim My Word even as I declared through My servant Malachi *(referring to Malachi 4:5–6)*.

The hearts of the older generation will turn to the younger. They will sincerely care for and empower them with love, nurture, and instruction.

The hearts of the younger generation will turn to the older. They will run alongside them with honor, respect, and grace, yet will be faithful and obedient to their own God-given calls and assignments.

Both generations will trumpet with one voice, a call to

prepare the way for My coming and to prepare the way for My Bride. Their voices in harmony will be filled with the spirit and power of Elijah.

The prophetic anointing they carry will expose and confront stumbling blocks that lead My people astray.

Those things that are high, lofty, and lifted up will be brought low.

Man's pride will be humbled, and the Lord alone will be exalted on that day.

The mountains will be brought low, and the valleys will be lifted up in the day when, in unity, the voices of the generations proclaim the preparation for the coming of the Lord.

In the days of John the Baptist, I raised up a prophet in Elijah's spirit and power to prepare the way of the Lord.

In these days, I am raising up a company in the spirit and power of Elijah to prepare the Bride for the coming of her Bridegroom.

This company represents both older and younger generations. Through My Spirit, they have turned their hearts to one another in love and respect and, therefore, will turn the hearts of many back to Me.

Great displays of power and majesty will be seen in the earth through this radical company of believers. Even as Elijah confronted the false prophets with a demonstration of power, so also will this company with a united voice confront the lies and assignments of the enemy who has deceived the masses. Power and glory will be restored to a remnant in My church, and many will believe and come to Me through this company that runs together. Like the prophets of Baal who bowed low through Elijah's confrontation, many who were trapped in deception will freely declare, "The Lord, He is God!"

The blessing will come with the alignment of hearts to Me and to each other. Curse is the alternative. The time is short. Prepare the way. Maranatha.

CONVERSATION POINT

How should believers respond to the call of the Lord to prepare the way as one voice?

ACTIVATION

What will you do and when?

About Patricia King

Patricia King is a respected apostolic and prophetic minister of the gospel. She is an accomplished itinerant speaker, author, television host, media producer, and ministry network overseer who has given her life fully to Jesus Christ and to His Kingdom's advancement in the earth.

She is the founder of Patricia King Ministries, Women in Ministry Network, and Everlasting Love Academy. She has written many books and has produced an abundance of resources on digital media. She is also a successful business owner and an inventive entrepreneur. Patricia's reputation in the Christian community is world-renowned.

To Connect:

Patricia King website: PatriciaKing.com

Women in Ministry Network: WIMNglobal.com

Facebook: Facebook.com/PatriciaKingPage

Instagram: PatriciaKingPage

YouTube: https://www.youtube.com/c/PatriciaKingPage

Patricia King Academy: EverlastingLoveAcademy.com

About Benjamin Deitrick

Benjamin Deitrick and his wife Tarrah are co-founders of Ignite Ministries International, based out of Maricopa, Arizona. Benjamin has given his life to full-time ministry for over two decades in various roles of service. He is a gifted, musician, prophet, teacher, author, and has also served in a pastoral and apostolic role in a local church.

As a seasoned minister, Benjamin has preached the word of God, delivered accurate prophetic ministry, and manifested diverse demonstrations of the Spirit in many cities and nations here and abroad. Benjamin and Tarrah have been married since 2010 and treasure their three beautiful daughters, Faith, Lily, and Sophia.

Website:

Igniteministriesinternational.com

More Books and Resources by Patricia King

Available at PatriciaKing.com

"Patricia King shows us a better way to live, overflowing with God's love instead of offense. *Live Unoffendable* is a must-read for this generation." —Dr. Ché Ahn

We are living in an era of division and offense. Almost everyone is on edge, ready to fight one another to the bitter end. This should not be so in the body of Christ, as there are few things that short-circuit our Kingdom calling and effectiveness for God quicker than offense. *Live Unoffendable* reveals the causes and consequences of offense and, even more importantly, shows you how to be free from this trap of darkness so that you can live a better way—a Kingdom way.

> As an added bonus, at the end of each chapter there is a QR code for a complimentary video with additional teaching and inspiration from Patricia.

More Books and Resources by Patricia King

Available at PatriciaKing.com

"This study has the power to change culture—first in the individual, then the home, the church, and ultimately society. This course is for everyone and I highly recommend it."

—Stacey Campbell

The Unoffendable Love Study Guide is based on the book *Live Unoffendable,* revealing the causes and damaging consequences of offense that are affecting the health and well-being of individuals, marriages, families, churches, workplaces, and entire regions and nations.

You will learn how to live free from this trap of darkness so you can live a better way, one that will establish the flow of God's goodness in and through your life!

You have the choice of two versions: One with the Study Outlines only, and another with QR codes that host full teachings for each lesson with both audio and video options.

More Books and Resources by Patricia King

Available at PatriciaKing.com

Decree the Word!

Decree a thing and it shall be established. — Job 22:28

Filled with powerful decrees from Scripture, *Decree* puts the Word of God to work in your life. When you start declaring them in the key areas of your life, get ready for the Kingdom to come and your breakthrough to manifest, because God's Word never returns void, and it accomplishes all it is sent to do! Areas of decree include favor, glory, blessing, health, prosperity, business, victory, wisdom, marriage, family, wealth, and many more!

God's Law of Attraction

Your soul is the epicenter of what happens in your life.

Patricia King takes you on a riveting journey through your soul to discover why, and, more importantly, how it holds the secret to a life of abundance and success. When your soul is aligned with God's promises and purposes, you can possess your destiny and live in the perpetual blessings of *God's Law of Attraction*.

More Books and Resources by Patricia King

Available at PatriciaKing.com

Your Best Years Are Ahead

Patricia exposes the lie that those in "the second half of life" are to slow down and check out as we grow older. She replaces it with the Kingdom truth that we are called to be full of vision, purpose, and productivity all the days of our life.

Full of scriptural insights, practical tips, and inspiring stories, *God's Anti-Aging Plan* will help you grab hold of a whole new way of living in the second half of life – a way that plugs you into God's Anti-Aging Plan so you can enjoy your best years in the years to come!

Narcissism Exposed

Patricia King delves into the psychological and spiritual roots of narcissism, a disorder that is running rampant in both the world and the church. As you read, you will learn what narcissism is and how it manifests, how it takes root in an individual, the truth about narcissism in the church today, how to live with someone who is under of influence of a spirit of narcissism, and much more. A must read!

Additional copies of this book and other
book titles from Patricia King are available at:

PatriciaKing.com
Amazon.com

Bulk/wholesale prices for stores and ministries:

Please contact: resource@PatriciaKing.com

www.ingramcontent.com/pod-product-compliance
Lightning Source LLC
Chambersburg PA
CBHW050846160426
43193CB00034B/1907